A LEGAL, CULTURAL, FACTUAL, THEOLOGICAL, AND BIBLICAL ANALYSIS OF THE JULY 13, 2024, ATTEMPTED ASSASSINATION OF DONALD JOHN TRUMP

A LEGAL, CULTURAL, FACTUAL, THEOLOGICAL, AND BIBLICAL ANALYSIS OF THE JULY 13, 2024, ATTEMPTED ASSASSINATION OF DONALD JOHN TRUMP

RELIGION AND LAW SERIES, VOLUME TEN

George J. Gatgounis

WIPF & STOCK · Eugene, Oregon

A Legal, Cultural, Factual, Theological, and Biblical Analysis of the July 13, 2024, Attempted Assassination of Donald John Trump

Religion and Law Series, Volume Ten

Resource Publications
An Imprint of Wipf and Stock Publishers
199 W. 8th Ave., Suite 3
Eugene, OR 97401

www.wipfandstock.com

PAPERBACK ISBN: 979-8-3852-4477-5
HARDCOVER ISBN: 979-8-3852-4478-2
EBOOK ISBN: 979-8-3852-4479-9

VERSION NUMBER 010926

DEDICATION

Alan M. Garber,

Harvard's 31st President

May he be granted wisdom in all things.

CONTENTS

ACKNOWLEDGEMENTS

Proofreading Editor: David C. Munday
Research Clerks/Paralegals:
Elizabeth Richmond Crofoot and Hannah Grace Lemacks
With gratitude for their contributions.

LEGAL ANALYSIS

Legal Restrictions on Speech Advocating Assassination of a President, Past or Present[1]

Prompted by the recent attempted assassination of former President Trump, questions about the scope of the Government's authority to prosecute threatening statements under federal law are apropos. Poignantly, over recent past years several celebrities have made flagrant public statements evoking violent imagery but have not been prosecuted. Kathy Griffin,[2] for instance, posted a photo to her social media of then-President Trump's bloody beheaded effigy held in her hand,[3] and Madonna stated during a speech that she "had visions of blowing up the White House."[4] Although both

---

1. In the treatment entitled "Legal Analysis," footnotes conform to the Harvard "Bluebook: A Uniform System of Citation" (22nd edition; May 2025 publication), except that theological references follow the *SBL Handbook of Style* (2nd ed. 2014), of the Society of Biblical Literature. *The Bluebook: A Uniform System of Citation* 22d ed. (Harvard Law Review Ass'n et al. eds. 2025) (cited hereafter as "Bluebook").

2. Joyce Chen, *Secret Service Investigating Kathy Griffin for Trump Scandal*, Rolling Stone (June 2, 2017), https://www.rollingstone.com/culture/culture-news/secret-service-investigating-kathy-griffin-for-trump-scandal-195623/.

3. Rebecca Rubin, Ted Johnson & Lawrence Yee, *Kathy Griffin Apologizes After Drawing Outrage for Beheading "Trump" in Photo*, Variety (May 30, 2017), https://variety.com/2017/tv/news/kathy-griffin-trump-beheading-photo-1202448058.

4. Christie D'Zuria, *Madonna Clarifies "Blowing Up the White House"*

women were indeed investigated by the Secret Service, neither was prosecuted.[5] Numerous celebrities have proffered public expressions of varieties of violence against a President—beating him up as in high school (Joe Biden), slugging him in the face (Robert De Niro), stabbing him (Shakespeare in the Park), clubbing him (Mickey Rourke), shooting him (Snoop Dogg), poisoning him (Anthony Bourdain), suffocating him (Larry Wilmore), bounty killing him (George Lopez), eating his flesh (Pearl Jam), blowing him up (Madonna, Moby), throwing him over a cliff (Rosie O'Donnell), martyring him (Reid Hoffman: "Yeah, I wish I had made him an actual martyr"), and assassinating him (Big Sean and Johnny Depp).[6]

Ironically, on the very day of the July 13, 2024, assassination attempt, President Joe Biden expostulated, "The idea that there's violence in America like this is just unheard of."[7] Orwellian double-speak is the norm in American politics—desire for violence is heard from thought leaders, then denied as if nothing of the kind was ever said.

Johnny Depp flippantly, bombastically, and unambiguously posited the rhetorical question, "When was the last time an actor assassinated a President?"[8] Depp later apologized: "It did not come out as intended, and I intended no malice. I was only trying to

---

Comment: "Taken Wildly Out of Context," L.A. Times (Jan. 23, 2017), https://www.latimes.com/entertainment/gossip/laetmgmadonnawomensmarchsecret-service20170123htmlstory.html.

5. Jennifer Deutschmann, Madonna: Speech Reportedly Sparks Secret Service Investigation, Yahoo News (Jan. 24, 2017), https://www.yahoo.com/news/madonna-speech-reportedly-sparks-secret-200712355.html.

6. Victor Davis Hanson, Assassination Porn and the Sickness on the Left, JNS (July 14, 2024), https://www.jns.org/assassination-porn-and-the-sickness-on-the-left/.

7. Al Jazeera Staff, Donald Trump Rally Shooting: MinutebyMinute Timeline of What Happened, Al Jazeera (July 14, 2024), https://www.aljazeera.com/news/2024/7/14/donald-trump-rally-shooting-minute-by-minute-timeline-of-what-happened.

8. Johnny Depp Apologizes for Donald Trump Assassination Joke, Variety (June 23, 2017), https://www.variety.com/2017/film/news/johnny-depp-trump-assassination-apology-1202477242/.

amuse, not to harm anyone."[9] 2578 days—or 7 years, 21 days, or 84 months, 21 days—later, inclusive, an assassin's bullet came within approximately one centimeter of publicly murdering a former President of the United States on live camera before a watching world. Some celebrities say what they want, then when challenged, do not want what they say.

Cases explored *infra* dissect the differentiation of a "true threat" from a hollow, non-lethal threat. Dividing "true" and actual threats from mere political puffery that pose no risk of harm is the task of a trial court as a tier of fact. As Professor Cary Coglianese of Harvard's Kennedy School echoed/quoted Professor Phil Heymann of Harvard Law: "all courts do . . . is draw lines."[10] These celebrities were not prosecuted as law enforcement considered the statements, investigated their context, and concluded the statements to be not a "true threat," only a rhetorical/political rebuke, and thus were protected by the First Amendment as political speech. Notwithstanding the immunities afforded by the First Amendment free-speech clause, all speech has consequences.[11] ". . . ὃ γὰρ ἐὰν σπείρῃ ἄνθρωπος, τοῦτο καὶ θερίσει."[12] Because whatever is sown is eventually reaped[13]—"what goes around comes around."[14]

9. Johnny Depp Apologizes for Donald Trump Assassination Joke, *Variety* (June 23, 2017), https://www.variety.com/2017/film/news/johnny-depp-trump-assassination-apology-1202477242/.

10. Unpublished class notes, Harvard Kennedy School of Government, Professor Cary Coglianese, quoting Professor Phil Heymann of Harvard Law School in STM "Law and Public Policy," Fall Semester '94.

11. ". . . ὃ γὰρ ἐὰν σπείρῃ ἄνθρωπος, τοῦτο καὶ θερίσει."; Kurt Aland et al., *The Greek New Testament, Fourth Revised Edition (Interlinear with Morphology)* (Deutsche Bibelgesellschaft, 1993), Gal. 6:7.

12. Kurt Aland et al., *The Greek New Testament, Fourth Revised Edition (Interlinear with Morphology)* (Deutsche Bibelgesellschaft, 1993), Gal. 6:7.

13. *The Holy Bible: King James Version*, Electronic Edition of the 1900 Authorized Version. (Bellingham, WA: Logos Research Systems, Inc., 2009), Gal. 6:7–8: "7 Be not deceived; God is not mocked: for whatsoever a man soweth, that shall he also reap. 8 For he that soweth to his flesh shall of the flesh reap corruption; but he that soweth to the Spirit shall of the Spirit reap life everlasting."

14. *Cf.* Kurt Aland et al., *The Greek New Testament, Fourth Revised Edition*

Threats of violence against the sitting President or Vice President of the United States are prohibited by 18 USC § 871(a). Consider the explicit restrictions of Title 18, Section 871(a) of the Federal Code, rendering threats liable for up to five (5) years imprisonment:

> Whoever knowingly and willfully deposits for convey-ance in the mail or for a delivery from any post office or by any letter carrier any letter, paper, writing, print, mis-sive, or document containing any threat to take the life of, to kidnap, or to inflict bodily harm upon the Presi-dent of the United States, the President-elect, the Vice President or other officer next in the order of succession to the office of President of the United States, or the Vice President-elect, or knowingly and willfully otherwise makes any such threat against the President, President-elect, Vice President or other officer next in the order of succession to the office of President, or Vice President-elect, shall be fined under this title or imprisoned not more than five years, or both.

Threats against any former President or Vice President, a member of their immediate families, a major candidate for President or Vice President, or any person protected by the Se-cret Service are prohibited under 18 USC § 879. Federal law also prohibits publishing threats against others, including prominent agency officials or even fellow social-media users.[15] The outer limit of what can be considered a threat under these statutes is defined by the First Amendment.[16] Under the current standard, speech is generally protected by the First Amendment unless such speech is "directed to inciting or producing imminent lawless action and is likely to incite or produce such action."[17] The case law separates the

---

(*Interlinear with Morphology*) (Deutsche Bibelgesellschaft, 1993), Gal. 6:7: " Μὴ πλανᾶσθε, θεὸς οὐ μυκτηρίζεται. ὃ γὰρ ἐὰν σπείρῃ ἄνθρωπος, τοῦτο καὶ θερίσει·"

15. 18 U.S.C. § 875 (2024).

16. *Watts v. United States*, 394 U.S. 705, 89 S. Ct. 1399, 22 L. Ed. 2d 664 (1969).

17. *Brandenburg v. Ohio*, 395 U.S. 444, 447, 89 S. Ct. 1827, 1829, 23 L. Ed. 2d 430 (1969).

colloquial idea of a threat from an actionable statement by the use of the term "true threat."

A "true threat" is a statement where the speaker means to express a serious intent to commit violence against a particular person or group.[18] The speaker does not need to actually intend to carry out his threat, as the purpose is to protect individuals from the fear of violence, including intimidation.[19] While not explicitly stated in case law, this standard suggests that there must be some level of capacity or ability to carry out the threat. A "true threat" must be an actual threat of violence, not a statement of hopeful or wishful thinking (i.e., "I hope they get him").[20] The landmark case on this issue is *Watts v. United States*, where a man attending a political rally in Washington, D.C., stated:[21]

> They always holler at us to get an education. And now I have already received my draft classification as 1-A and I have got to report for my physical this Monday coming. I am not going. If they ever make me carry a rifle the first man I want to get in my sights is L. B. J. They are not going to make me kill my black brothers.

The court ultimately found that there was no "true threat" because the statements were made during a political debate, expressly conditioned on the defendant's entry into the Army, and the participants in the conversation laughed and joked after the statement was made.[22] The defendant's statement was determined to be "political hyperbole" that may be crude and offensive but was nonetheless protected by the free speech clause of the First Amendment.[23] The court began with the First Amendment protections and reasoned

18. *Virginia v Black*, 538 U.S. 343, 358; 123 S. Ct. 1536; 155 L. Ed. 2d 535 (2003).

19. *Id.* at 359.

20. *Rankin v. McPherson*, 483 U.S. 378, 107 S. Ct. 2891, 97 L. Ed. 2d 315 (1987).

21. *Watts v. United States*, 394 U.S. 705, 89 S. Ct. 1399, 22 L. Ed. 2d 664 (1969).

22. *Id.* at 707.

23. *Id.* at 708.

that the statement must be taken in context and that the language of debate is often sharp and unpleasant but that debate on public issues should be unhindered.[24]

In a more recent case, a district court sitting in the Fourth Circuit was asked to restrain a defendant from making threatening statements about the plaintiff's counsel in litigation arising out of the 2017 Unite the Right Rally in Charlottesville.[25] The defendant made threatening remarks[26] on Telegram, a social-media site, about plaintiff's counsel in the midst of a series of ongoing legal proceedings regarding the defendant's communications on social media and participation in the 2017 Unite the Right rally.[27] The defendant posted an article about the plaintiff's attorney and her work overturning the federal ban on same-sex marriages with the statement, "[a]fter this stupid kike whore loses this fraudulent law-suit, we're going to have a lot of fucking fun with her."[28] The plain-tiff requested a court order enjoining the defendant from making any further threats, alleging that, "Cantwell's post went beyond menacing and offensive language: it was a thinly veiled threat to harm Ms. Kaplan . . . and to encourage others to harm her," due to her involvement in this lawsuit.[29] The court disagreed, finding that the statement "comes close to—but does not cross—the line between protected speech and a true threat of physical violence."[30] The court reasoned that the defendant's statement did not show any intent to physically harm or kill anyone and the statement could be seen as a threat to denigrate the plaintiff on social media

24. *Id.*

25. *Sines v. Kessler*, No. 3:17-cv-00072, 2020 U.S. Dist. LEXIS 94254, at *9 (W.D. Va. May 29, 2020) (involving ten Charlottesville residents as Plaintiffs against organizers and sponsors of the 2017 Unite the Right rally, alleging viola-tions as well 42 U.S.C. § 1985 as well as related state laws, seeking damages and injunctive relief).

26. *Sines v. Kessler*, No. 3:17-cv-00072, 2020 U.S. Dist. LEXIS 94254, at *9 (W.D. Va. May 29, 2020).

27. *Id.* at *10.

28. *Id.*

29. *Id.* at *11.

30. *Id.* at *18.

and thus was not a threat at all.[31] Further, the defendant's statement was conditioned on winning the lawsuit, indicating that any action would not be imminent.[32]

Where a "true threat" has been found, the statements generally threatened imminent violence against a person covered by statute, were not political in nature, and evidenced an intent to be viewed as a threat.[33] In *U.S. v. Rogers,* a jury found a "true threat" where the defendant made threatening statements in a hotel restaurant towards then-President Nixon, who was in China at the time.[34] Specifically, the defendant stated he was going to walk to Washington to "whip Nixon's ass" or "kill him in order to save the United States."[35] The jury was permitted to convict based on a showing that a reasonable man would have foreseen that the statements would be viewed as a threat.[36]

Notwithstanding the egregious threat, rather than address the propriety of that standard, the Supreme Court reversed the conviction based on a violation of Rule 43 of the Federal Rules of Criminal Procedure, which requires the defendant to be present at all critical stages of the prosecution. The Supreme Court found that the jury's question "whether the court would 'accept the Verdict—Guilty as charged with extreme mercy of the Court'"[37]— should have been communicated to the defendant and the jury should have been reminded that their recommendation was not binding. However, Justice Marshall stated in his concurrence that

31. *Id.* at *19–20.

32. *Id.* at *20.

33. *United States v. Rogers,* 488 F.2d 512 (5th Cir. 1974), rev'd on other grounds, 422 U.S. 35 (1975) (reversed trial court, and Fifth Circuit, which convicted under 18 U.S.C §871(a)); *United States v. Kosma,* 951 F.2d 549 (3d Cir. 1991) (convicting Defendant under 18 U.S.C. § 871 for mailing letters threatening to harm President Reagan); *United States v. Ziobrowski,* No. 18–10250-DJC, 2019 U.S. Dist. LEXIS 122141 (D. Mass. July 23, 2019) (convicting Defendant under 18 U.S.C. § 871 for issuing threats through interstate commerce).

34. *Rogers,* 488 F.2d at 513.

35. *Rogers,* 422 U.S. at 42 (Marshall, J., concurring).

36. *Id.* at 44 (Marshall, J., concurring).

37. *Id.* at 36.

he would have reversed as well, but on the merits of the case.[38] In his concurrence, Justice Marshall cautioned that the objective, reasonable person approach employed by the District Court embodied a negligence standard which should be avoided for criminal statutes.[39] Years later, analyzing the similarly worded 18 USC § 875(c), involving threats against any person, the Supreme Court ruled that the reasonable person standard is inappropriate and the person making the statement must be aware of the threatening nature of the communication.[40]

Where there is no political context or audience for the statements, it is more likely that a "true threat" will be found.[41] The defendant in *Kosma* mailed a postcard to President Reagan at the White House that stated[42]:

> Mr. Reagan: You are hereby invited to PHILADELPHIA. We are going to give you a 21 Gun-Salute. 21 guns are going to put bullets thru your heart & brains. You are a Disgrace to the Air-Force. You are a Disgrace to Teddy Roosevelt. You are a Disgrace to John F. Kennedy. You a Disgrace to Nancy Reagan. You have insulted her intelligence, and dignity, and honor, and integrity, and I resent this very much.!! You are In Contempt of EVERYTHING that I represent, and standby, and believe. Officially: an Act of Contempt of Court. Your name is going to be removed from ALL documents, and books. OFFICIALLY: you were NEVER the "president" of anything.!!

The defendant also sent a series of letters to a presidential assistant, stating that the letter should not have been intercepted and that

---

38. *Id.* at 43 (Marshall, J., concurring).

39. *Id.* at 47 (Marshall, J., concurring).

40. *Elonis v. United States*, 575 U.S. 723, 739, 135 S. Ct. 2001, 2011 (2015); 18 USC § 875(c) states, "[w]hoever transmits in interstate or foreign commerce any communication containing any threat to kidnap any person or any threat to injure the person of another, shall be fined under this title or imprisoned not more than five years, or both."

41. *Kosma*, 951 F.2d 549.

42. *Id.* at 550.

the President does not know he has been sentenced to death.[43] A final letter was sent to the now former President Reagan while the defendant was awaiting trial and the defendant was also charged under 18 USC § 879.[44]

Although the defendant only appealed the conviction under § 871, regarding threats of violence against the President, the court noted that the test under § 879, for threats against, *inter alia*, a former President, was more akin to the subjective standard originally advocated by Justice Marshall and later adopted by the Supreme Court in *Elonis*.[45] 18 USC § 879 is not frequently cited and courts appear to be split as to whether § 871 and § 879 are evaluated under the same standard.[46]

Contrasting the *Kosma* case with *Watts*, the court found the statements in the postcard and letters were true threats actionable under § 871 for multiple reasons: (1) there was no political context, (2) the statements were not conditional, and (3) the only audience was the President.[47] In *Watts*, the threats were made at a political rally, conditioned on the speaker joining the Army, and made to a small audience of rally attendants who all laughed afterward.[48] While framed as an "invitation," the statements were not conditional as they were in *Watts*, as some of the letters named a specific time and date for the "21 gun salute."[49] The only audience here was the President (and White House staff) and nobody was laughing after receiving the letters.[50]

In a more recent case analyzing 18 USC § 875(c), the statute address in *Elonis*, the Fourth Circuit found that a violent tweet

43. *Id.* at 551.

44. *Id.* at 552.

45. *Id.* at 556; *Elonis*, 575 U.S. 739.

46. *Elonis v. United States*, 575 U.S. 723, 739, 135 S. Ct. 2001, 2011 (2015) (requiring subjective intent, not mere negligence, for liability under 18 U.S.C. § 875(c); *United States v. Johnson*, 14 F.3d 766, 771 (2d Cir. 1994).

47. *Kosma*, 951 F.2d at 554.

48. *Watts*, 394 U.S. at 706.

49. *Kosma*, at 554.

50. *Id.*

published online constituted a true threat.[51] The tweet contained a photo of a lynching and stated, "HI PEDOPHILE PROPHET MUHAMMAD CUBE WORSHIPPING INBRED MUSLIM SCUM LETS MEET SO YOU CAN RUN THAT COWARD MOUTH TO MY FACE. . .PLEASE. . .VIEW YOUR DESTINY."[52] The court compared this to the communication in *Watts*, finding that the tweet was not posted in jest, was intended only for one person (although it was posted publicly), did not invite public discourse on religion, and when taken in context would appear to be a threat to a reasonable person.[53]

In summary, only "true threats" are prohibited by federal criminal statutes. For a statement to be a "true threat" there must be some effort by the speaker to communicate an intent to kill or physically injure another.[54] The analysis must start with the First Amendment, as a statement is presumed to be protected unless it is a "true threat" outside the protections of freedom of speech.[55] Vague allusions to possible violence,[56] expressing a wish for someone else to commit violence,[57] and conditional suppositions are generally insufficient to establish probable cause.

Where/How Has the U.S. Supreme Court Drawn the Line on Permissible Use of Lethal Force

The recent tragic assassination attempt on the life of the former President raises the issue of when law enforcement may use lethal force. Most dispositive to determine permissible parameters of the use of lethal force is *Graham v. Connor*, 490 U.S. 386, 109 S. Ct.

---

51. *United States v. Vandevere*, 849 F. App'x 69, 70–71 (4th Cir. 2021) (per curiam).

52. *United States v. Vandevere*, No. 1:19-cr-63-MOC, 2019 U.S. Dist. LEXIS 157692, at *1 (W.D.N.C. Sep. 16, 2019).

53. *Vandevere*, 849 F. App'x. at 71.

54. *Virginia v. Black*, supra note 9.

55. *Watts*, supra note 11; *Kosma*, supra note 31.

56. *Sines*, supra note 15.

57. *Rankin*, supra note 10.

1865 (1989). Under *Graham v. Connor*, 490 U.S. 386, 109 S. Ct. 1865 (1989), a law-enforcement sniper may use lethal force in situations similar to the recent attempted assassination of former president Donald Trump at the political rally in Butler, Pennsylvania. The assassination attempt involved an armed individual, Thomas Matthew Crooks, positioned on the roof of the AGR building at approximately 153 yards, who fired multiple rounds from an "AR-15 style" or "AR-15 type" rifle, killing an audience member and critically wounding two others, before a law-enforcement sniper fatally shot him with one round.

The factors that courts consider to determine if an officer's use of deadly force is justified are (1) the severity of the crime, (2) if the suspect poses an immediate threat to the safety of the officers or others, and (3) if the suspect is actively resisting arrest or attempting to flee.[58] In *Graham*, the Supreme Court determined that an "objective reasonableness" standard under the Fourth Amendment applies when deciding if a law-enforcement official used excessive force when making an arrest, during an investigatory stop, or during a "seizure" of a person.[59] When analyzing these claims, the court must pay "careful attention to the facts and circumstances of each particular case."[60] To determine the "reasonableness," the court must judge the conduct "from the perspective of a reasonable officer on the scene, rather than with the 20/20 vision of hindsight."[61] As explained in *Graham*, these are the three (3) factors courts consider when evaluating claims of excessive force.

In *Harris v. Roderick*, 126 F.3d 1189 (9th Cir. 1997), the Ninth Circuit found that qualified immunity did not apply when a sniper shot a suspect who did not pose an immediate threat to the officer or others. Multiple events transpired over two days, beginning with the United States Marshals entering property to serve an arrest warrant.[62] A Marshal shot and killed the property owner's dog,

58. *Graham*, 490 U.S. at 396, 109 S. Ct. at 1872.
59. *Id.* at 388, 109 S. Ct. at 1867.
60. *Id.* at 396, 109 S. Ct. at 1872.
61. *Id.*
62. *Id.* at 1193.

which prompted gunfire from the owner's son, and resulted in the death of the son and another Marshal.[63] A hostage-rescue team, which included a sniper, was later dispatched with a Special Rule of Engagement that any armed adult male could and should be killed.[64] The sniper shot the property owner in the back when he was outside and shot another bullet that killed the owner's wife and injured the plaintiff.[65] The plaintiff filed suit, alleging violations of his Fourth, Fifth, and Sixth Amendment rights.[66] The district court granted the defendants' motion to dismiss in part, based on qualified immunity, and the defendants appealed.

One of the issues under the consideration of the court was involved the "Special Rules," whether they violated the constitutional requirements.[67] The court reviewed *Graham*, 490 U.S. 386, 109 S. Ct. 1865, which held that reasonableness is not determined from hindsight but is determined from the reasonable perspective of the officer on the scene.[68] The court stated that "[l]aw enforcement officers may not shoot to kill unless, at a minimum, the suspect presents an immediate threat to the officer or others, or is fleeing and his escape will result in a serious threat of injury to persons."[69] The Special Rules adjudicated in *Harris v. Roderick*, 126 F.3d 1189 (9th Cir. 1997), that mandated the killing of any armed adult male, was deemed an unconstitutional use of force and an unjustified extreme order.[70]

The sniper in *Harris v. Roderick* argued that his use of force was objectively reasonable and any law to the contrary was not established.[71] The court determined that the sniper's actions did not pass the *Graham* test because deadly force is not permitted to kill

63. *Id.*

64. *Id.*

65. *Id.* at 1193–94.

66. *Id.* at 1194.

67. *Id.* at 1201.

68. *Harris*, 126 F.3d at 1201.

69. *Id.*

70. *Id.* at 1202.

71. *Id.*

a suspect who made no threatening movements and was running back to a cabin, even considering the earlier events.[72] The sniper gave no warning and no chance to surrender before shooting.[73] The plaintiff's recent violent crimes were not a justification for the shooting.[74] The court stated that "[l]aw enforcement officials may not kill suspects who do not pose an immediate threat to their safety or to the safety of others simply because they are armed."[75] The Ninth Circuit held the officers were not entitled to qualified immunity and affirmed the district court's decision.[76]

In *Aden v. City of Eagan*,[77] a foot chase ended with the suspect sitting on a curb and negotiators trying to get him to put his gun down. The suspect eventually set the gun down and, without the negotiators' knowledge, the officers launched a surprise assault maneuver that caused the suspect to reach for his gun and caused the officers, including two snipers, to shoot him dead.[78] The surprise tactical plan intended to use less-lethal force of flashbangs and foam rounds to cause the suspect to lean away from his gun on the ground.[79] The suspect previously had pointed a gun at a victim, fled the scene, fired his gun, and broke through a police barrier, but also had been sitting on the curb for hours without moving or

72. *Id.*

73. *Id.* at 1203.

74. *Id.*

75. *Id.* at 1204.

76. *Id.* at 1205.

77. *Aden v. City of Eagan*, Civ. No. 20–1508 (JWB/TNL), 2023 U.S. Dist. LEXIS 174925, at *1–2 (D. Minn. Sept. 29, 2023), reversed *Aden v. City of Eagan*, No. 233391, 2025 U.S. App. LEXIS ___ (8th Cir. Feb. 12, 2025) (holding that this § 1983 wrongful-death action, qualified immunity applies to the officers because firing occurred only after the decedent, Isak Aden, grabbed his weapon, Minnesota official immunity protects both the officers and City (vicarious immunity), and Monell liability against the City was properly dismissed, as there was no constitutional violation by any official). See lexipol.com+9law.justia.com+9ecf. ca8.uscourts.gov+9.

78. *Id.*

79. *Id.* at *15.

threatening anyone.[80] With regard to the reasonableness of the officer's use of less-lethal force and lethal force, the court determined that the use of less-lethal force was not objectively reasonable as a matter of law and there were questions of material fact that precluded granting the defendants' motion for summary judgment.[81] The court also determined that there were material questions of fact on the use of lethal force as to whether the suspect pointed his gun at the officers to put them under the immediate threat of serious harm and those questions precluded summary judgment.[82]

In another case with a differing fact pattern, *State v. White*, 2013-Ohio-51, ¶ 61 n.13, 988 N.E.2d 595, 614 n.13 (Ct. App. 2013), an Ohio appellate court noted in a footnote that deadly force may be used in an escape circumstance where the suspect's mere presence at large is an inherent danger to others.[83] The court further noted an example of this where a police sniper located a distance away may use deadly force when there is "no imminent, proximal threat to the officer taking action."[84] The facts in *White* involved an officer shooting during a traffic stop.[85]

Many cases that addressed a sniper's use of deadly force involved standoffs with a suspect. The Sixth Circuit held in *Messer v. Ind. State Police* that a sniper's use of excessive force was reasonable when the suspect aimed his gun because the suspect's previous actions showed that he posed a serious threat to the officers where there had been an armed standoff, the suspect set buildings on fire, his accomplice shot at a helicopter, and he was armed with a rifle.[86] The Northern District of Indiana held that the defendants'

80. *Id.* at *16–17.

81. *Id.* at *21.

82. *Id.* at *35–36.

83. *State v. White*, 2013-Ohio-51, ¶ 61 n.13, 988 N.E.2d 595, 614 n.13 (Ct. App. 2013).

84. *Id.*

85. *Id.*

86. *Livermore v. Lubelan*, 476 F.3d 397, 401 (6th Cir. 2007) (approving a segmented approach to excessive-force claims, emphasizing that officers' pre-seizure conduct is analyzed separately from the seizure itself). See law.justia.com+5opn. ca6.uscourts.gov+5ballotpedia.s3.amazonaws.com+5.

use of deadly force was reasonable and granted the defendants' motion for summary judgment on the federal claims after a two-hour standoff with a suspect who raised his gun and aimed at the officers.[87] In *Messer*, multiple officers fired their weapons at the suspect, but the sniper fired the deadly shot.[88]

Other courts also have addressed the use of a sniper after a standoff. In *Dixon v. Ga. Dep't of Pub. Safety*, No. 2:14-cv-47, 2018 U.S. Dist. LEXIS 65522 (S.D. Ga. Apr. 18, 2018), a sniper had probable cause to believe the suspect posed a threat of serious harm before firing on the suspect who was surrounded and walked to his running truck with a shotgun. The ruling in *Thomas v. Cannon*, Nos. 3:15–05346 BJR; 3:16-cv-05392, 2017 U.S. Dist. LEXIS 80800 (W.D. Wash. May 25, 2017) denied summary judgment for defendants after finding questions of fact whether the suspect was actually choking his child when he was shot by a sniper. In *Long v. City & County of Honolulu*, 511 F.3d 901 (9th Cir. 2007), an officer was objectively reasonable when and where he shot the suspect after the suspect shot several guests, refused to surrender, and officers reported that the suspect fired at them. It was immaterial whether the suspect actually fired because the officer heard a radio transmission about shots being fired and saw the suspect point a rifle. In *Cato v. County of San Bernardino*, No. 5:20-cv-02602-FWS-SHK, 2023 U.S. Dist. LEXIS 114370 (C.D. Cal. July 3, 2023), the trial court found reasonable the conduct of an officer where the suspect was engaged in a standoff, took a shooting stance, and fired his weapon. In *Liebenstein v. Crowe*, 826 F. Supp. 1174 (E.D. Wis. 1992), the court found the use of force to be reasonable where an officer shot the suspect while in a neighbor's house and where the suspect was mentally and emotionally unstable, firing his gun from the yard. In *Tauke v. Stine*, 120 F.3d 1363 (8th Cir. 1997), the adjudicating court, as a finder of fact, concluded the use of force to be reasonable by a sniper where a gunfight ensued when officers tried to arrest the suspect.

---

87. *Messer v. Ind. State Police*, 586 F. Supp. 2d 1044, 1047 (N.D. Ind. 2008).

88. *Id.* at 1055.

Estate of Smart v. City of Wichita, 951 F.3d 1161 (10th Cir. 2020) did not involve a sniper but did involve an active shooter. Crowds of people were leaving a concert venue and bars when gunshots were heard and people began running.[89] Officers shot and killed the decedent while he was running away.[90] The 10th Circuit found that while a jury could determine that the officers were mistaken when they thought the decedent was the active shooter and they could also determine that the mistake was unreasonable. The 10th Circuit found there was no clearly established law to put the officers on notice that their actions were unconstitutional.[91] The 10th Circuit affirmed the district court's grant of summary judgment in part, but reversed the grant of summary judgment due to a question of fact regarding the plaintiff's claim that some of the shots were fired after the decedent was no longer a threat.[92]

Cases considered *infra* have no identical, but in varying degrees similar, fact patterns to the recent assassination attempt. However, the cases reviewed above do involve at least some of the relevant facts and provide some examples of when law enforcement may use lethal force in certain situations. As the use of excessive force has been found reasonable in situations involving aiming a gun at officers or firing a gun, the use of excessive force here, where an armed and active shooter on top of a roof had already fired shots, would also be found reasonable.[93]

Conclusion

Whether Title 18, U.S.C. Sections 871, 875, and 879 would have been applied more rigorously by law enforcement, and potentially by courts of original jurisdiction, to any but "tefloned" celebrities remains an open question. These protective statues in our laws are

89. *Id.* at 1166.

90. *Id.*

91. *Id.* at 1174.

92. *Id.* at 1178.

93. See *Livermore*, 476 F.3d 397; *Messer*, 586 F. Supp. 2d 1044; *Cato*, 2023 U.S. Dist. LEXIS 114370; *Liebenstein*, 826 F. Supp. 1174; *Tauke*, 120 F.3d 1363.

"detoothed" if unwritten castes within our social structure are immunized. Fourteenth Amendment "equal protection" under the law necessitates the fairness of equal application of the law "without fear or favor."

As to the application of *Graham vs. Connor* in the (presently known[94]) fact pattern of the recent tragic but failed assassination attempt on the life of a former President, and current candidate for the same office, the parameters of this controlling, guiding Supreme Court case are unmistakable—a "clear and present danger," immediate, and unambiguous. The law-enforcement sniper was justified in taking the neutralizing, fatal shot as per the *Graham vs. Connor* "objective reasonableness"[95] standard.[96]

---

94. This manuscript was first submitted on December 15, 2024.

95. *Graham*, 490 U.S. at 396, 109 S. Ct. at 1867, 1872.

96. Questions of (1) whether the alleged 16–17 second delay in the firing of the fatal, neutralizing shot was negligence, (2) whether the law-enforcement snipers were ordered to stand down when the assassin was first spotted on the AGR building roof for a significant amount of time (alleged over 34 minutes even before the target ascended the stage), and (3) whether some law enforcement were not merely negligent but willfully so, remains to be investigated by House and Senate committees, as well as internal local police and Secret Service. Further, if the estate of the deceased Corey Comperatore sued local and Secret Service law enforcement under Section 1983, the family of the deceased as plaintiffs would be granted FRCP Rule 33 and 34 discovery rights.

CULTURAL ANALYSIS

When a Culture Goes Lunatic

Cultures[1] are biological—they are born, grow, ail, decline, and perish. The 19th-century English anthropologist Edward Burnett Tylor in the first paragraph of his *Primitive Culture* (1871) defined culture as follows:

> Culture . . . is that complex whole which includes knowledge, belief, art, morals, law, custom, and any other capabilities and habits acquired by man as a member of society.[2]

---

1. † In the treatment of "Cultural Analysis," footnotes conform to the *Publication Manual of the American Psychological Association* (7th ed. 2020), except that theological references follow the *SBL Handbook of Style* (2nd ed. 2014), of the Society of Biblical Literature.

Brittanica remarks that culture is "behaviour peculiar to *Homo sapiens*, together with material objects used as an integral part of this behaviour. Thus, culture includes language, ideas, beliefs, customs, codes, institutions, tools, techniques, works of art, rituals, and ceremonies, among other elements." Leslie A. White. (n.d.). *Culture*, in *Encyclopaedia Britannica*. Retrieved July 15, 2025, from https://www.britannica.com/topic/culture.

2. Tylor, E. B. (1871). *Primitive culture: Researches into the development of mythology, philosophy, religion, language, art and custom* (Vols. 1–2). London: John Murray.

The "complex whole"[3] can become better—or worse. Some cultures become sicker than others. Some cultures degenerate into stages where taking the life of the ruler is deemed a justifiable palliative. As Dorman Eaton in 1881 opined on tragic decline:

> Civilization has its stages at which the taking of the life of a ruler is held a justifiable remedy in politics. Tyrannicide was defended in Greece. The bloody work of Brutus and Cassius was not generally condemned except by the adherents of Cæsar. A man might defend his country as he might his own life, by taking that of its enemy. The fearful experience of half the nations of Europe in our own time discloses great elements of population ready to justify the savage remedy of the assassin when passions are up or a sense of wrong maddens the people.[4]

A "sense of wrong"[5] may turn some cultures upward, as the Whitfieldian/Wesleyan revivals on both sides of the Atlantic in the 1740s progressed into what would be called the Methodist Revival, and in America, the Great Awakening. A "sense of wrong" turned the British and American cultures of the 1740's upward. Obversely, a "sense of wrong" may depress, degenerate, and descend a culture to savagery.

As Dorman Eaton further opines regarding "ominous indications" of declension, when "a sense of wrong maddens the people":

> Those we call lunatics are often little more than ill-balanced intellects, reasoning and deciding rather according to the standards of earlier times and a lower civilization than our own; yet with so much justice and logic that, while doubting their responsibility, we recognize their acts as ominous indications. In whatever walk of life insanity increases, we expect to find great wrongs or gross violations of morality.[6]

3. *Id.*

4. Eaton, D. B. (1881). Assassination and the spoils system. *The Princeton Review*, 2, 145. See https://ref.ly/logosres/princrevo4?ref=VolumePage.V+2%2c+p+145&off=36&ctx=D+THE+SPOILS+SYSTEM~CIVILIZATION+has+its.

5. *Id.*

6. Eaton, D. B. (1881). Assassination and the spoils system. *The Princeton*

An "ill-balanced" lunatic turned assassin reasoned according to the obtuse standards of political savagery. The spoils of assassination are poisonous, infectious fruits. Indeed, "μικρὰ ζύμη ὅλον τὸ φύραμα ζυμοῖ."[7]/ "A little leaven leaveneth the whole lump"—it is the nature of political evil to spread. When in politics, "insanity increases, we expect to find great wrongs . . ."[8] "These are times that try men's souls."[9]

In 1971 Don McClean released his iconic commentary in song on the degeneration of American culture—the hit of hits "American Pie." Perceiving the cultural paradigm shift downward, the loss of moorings on historic American ideological underpinnings, and the change from a theistic focus to earthly, McClean captured the feel of a new darkness, where "Father, Son, and Holy Ghost" "took the last train for the coast."[10] The following adaption of his lyrics might have been his rhyme at the site of the tragic attempt assassination, where perhaps, "Satan" was "laughing with delight":

> . . . the three [edited; as per Third Commandment] I ad-
> mire most, Father, Son, and the Holy Ghost . . . caught
> the last train for the coast . . .[11]

McClean remarks that he could not "remember" if he "cried," when he "read about those who died." Poetically, philosophically, "and

---

Review, 2, 145. See https://ref.ly/logosres/princrev04?ref=VolumePage.V+2%2c+ p+145&off=36&ctx=D+THE+SPOILS+SYSTEM~CIVILIZATION+has+its.

7. Kurt Aland et al., *The Greek New Testament, Fourth Revised Edition (with Morphology)* (Deutsche Bibelgesellschaft, 1993; 2006), Ga 5:9.

8. Eaton, D. B. (1881). Assassination and the spoils system. *The Princeton Review*, 2, 145. See https://ref.ly/logosres/princrev04?ref=VolumePage.V+2%2c+ p+145&off=36&ctx=D+THE+SPOILS+SYSTEM~CIVILIZATION+has+its.

9. Paine, T. (1776). *The American Crisis* (No. 1). Boston: [Author]. Retrieved from https://www.loc.gov/item/2020774926/.

10. Adapted from McLean, D. (1971). *American Pie* [Song]. On *American Pie*. United Artists Records.

11. Adapted from McLean, D. (1971). *American Pie* [Song]. On *American Pie*. United Artists Records.

here politically, "something touched" "deep inside" . . . .[12] McClean perhaps would have "cried"[13] on July 13, 2024.

The Culture of Heroism—The Christian Father Martyr

Amidst cultural degeneration, individuals may stand as vanguards of heroism. Corey Comperatore "died a hero," as he "was the very best of us," said Pennsylvania Gov. Josh Shapiro, the day after the brave firefighter, his trained instincts triggered to protect others' lives before his own, sacrificed himself to take gunfire from the assassin. Mr. Comperatore, of Sarver, Pa., had two daughters, Allyson, 27, and Kaylee, 24. Fellow firefighter and friend Jeff Lowers remarked that Comperatore's "quick instincts" appeared to come into play during the shooting.[14]

"Being a volunteer fireman, no matter what you're doing, when the whistle goes off and the monitor goes off, you go and do what you need to do," said his colleague and friend Jeff Lowers.[15] Dr. James Sweetland, an emergency-room physician at the rally, rushed to help Mr. Comperatore after he was shot. He said that Mr. Comperatore was "lying in a pool of blood," and two people helped lift him onto a bench so the physician could give CPR. Another attendee rushed to put pressure on Mr. Comperatore's wound above his ear, but Dr. Sweetland said there was no pulse. Two Pennsylvania State troopers helped lift Mr. Comperatore onto a stretcher,[16]

---

12. Adapted from McLean, D. (1971). *American Pie* [Song]. On *American Pie.* United Artists Records.

13. Adapted from McLean, D. (1971). *American Pie* [Song]. On *American Pie.* United Artists Records.

14. Londono, E., Taft, I., Morales, C., & Conway, B. (2024, July 14). *Corey Comperatore, victim in Trump shooting, remembered for his faith and bravery.* The New York Times. See https://www.nytimes.com/2024/07/14/us/corey-comperatore-trump-shooting-victim.html.

15. Londono, E., Taft, I., Morales, C., & Conway, B. (2024, July 14). *Corey Comperatore, victim in Trump shooting, remembered for his faith and bravery.* The New York Times. See https://www.nytimes.com/2024/07/14/us/corey-comperatore-trump-shooting-victim.html.

16. Londono, E., Taft, I., Morales, C., & Conway, B. (2024, July 14). *Corey*

as he had made his last call of duty. "Greater love hath no man than this, that a man lay down his life . . ." (John 15:13).[17]

The Culture of Altruism—A Former First Lady's Call to Reason

Melania Trump, former First Lady, was quick to respond with an *apropos* public statement: "America, the fabric of our gentle nation is tattered, but our courage and common sense must ascend and bring us back together as one." She exuded empathy to the suffering victims: "Your need to summon your inner strength for such a terrible reason saddens me." She summoned all to consider inner humanity, not to be obscured by the "political machine." "The core facets of my husband's life—his human side—were buried below the political machine." She skillfully painted the daubs of bitter darkness, but pierced the darkness with a sharp beam of light: "Dawn is here again. Let us unite. Now." Her message that behind every politician, regardless of positions, is a human with a loving family undercut the bitterness of the exteriority of American politics.

The Culture of Violent Sociopathology—A "Non-Overt" Political Assassin

The assassin's identity appeared, on the exterior surface, to be bland—not the expected, vitriolic, violent, and vengeful persona of one the wife of the victim referred to as a "monster." The assassin Thomas Crooks, born September 20, 2003, age 20, may have been taken to be just another young guy making it through college with a side job, had he not chosen the path of public political violence.

Comperatore, victim in Trump shooting, remembered for his faith and bravery. The New York Times. See https://www.nytimes.com/2024/07/14/us/corey-comperatore-trump-shooting-victim.html.

17. *The Holy Bible: King James Version*, Electronic Edition of the 1900 Authorized Version. (Bellingham, WA: Logos Research Systems, Inc., 2009), John 15:13–14.

Jason Kohler, former classmate of the shooter at Bethel Park High School, identified the shooter as "a total loner" who was "bullied" constantly. Crooks wore a mask even after the Covid crisis had passed. Kohler was clear "he was an outcast, isolated." When asked by NBC 4 Washington if his past ostracism contributed to what he did in the assassination, Kohler could not connect the dots.[18] Dan Gryzbeck, Crooks' city councilman, remarked that his mother is a Democrat and his father a Libertarian.[19]

The overt politics of the assassin did not belay one who would lose his life in pursuit of taking another's. Although registered a Republican, Crooks donated $15 to the Progressive Turnout Project, through the Democrat donation platform ActBlue in January 2021. His overt political connections did not belie the violence of vengeance nor vitriol.[20] According to the *Tribune-Review* of western Pennsylvania, Crooks won the $500 "Star Award" from the National Math and Science Initiative, thus indicating focus as a student.

Sociopathology is not the sole province of the assassin. Alex Jones poured his own sociopathology: "It was the Deep State! . . . and they will also try to kill Biden!" Jones alleged that the ever-looming governmental Leviathan—"They"—want to create bedlam so that emergency powers may be invoked and totalitarian rule assumed. Victor Davis Hanson opines upon political sociopathology of the left, "We have witnessed for years blatant exceptions to the once common custom that we don't normalize the imagined killing of any president or presidential candidate and thus lower the bar of violence."[21] Hanson alleges the Left has "anomalized" Trump, making him an exception to the heretofore general consensus that killing a President is morally reprehensible. "But the

18. Jason Kohler, interview by author, NBC 4 Washington, offsite.

19. Baker, M., Bogel-Burroughs, N., Conway, B., & Ericson, M. (2024, July 14). *The New York Times*. Jack Begg contributed research.

20. Baker, M., Bogel-Burroughs, N., Conway, B., & Ericson, M. (2024, July 14). *The New York Times*. Jack Begg contributed research.

21. Hanson, V. D. (2024, July 15). *Assassination porn and the sickness on the left*. Jewish News Syndicate. https://www.jns.org/assassination-porn-and-the-sickness-on-the-left/.

Left constantly makes Trump an exception. Now, it is as if the imagined killing of Trump had been mainstreamed and become acceptable in a way inconceivable of other presidents." Consider, in contradistinction, a rodeo clown who wore an Obama mask in a bull-riding contest at the Missouri State Fair. The individual was publicly punished, banned permanently by the Missouri State Fair authorities. Hanson describes sociopathic "parlor games" among celebrities hopefully merely joking about inflicting bodily harm— "by slugging his face (Robert De Niro), by decapitation (Kathy Griffin, Marilyn Manson), by stabbing (Shakespeare in the Park), by clubbing (Mickey Rourke), by shooting (Snoop Dogg), by poisoning (Anthony Bourdain), by bounty killing (George Lopez), by carrion eating his corpse (Pearl Jam), by suffocating (Larry Wilmore), by blowing him up (Madonna, Moby), by throwing him over a cliff (Rosie O'Donnell), just by generic "killing" him (Johnny Depp, Big Sean), or by martyring him (Reid Hoffman: "Yeah, I wish I had made him an actual martyr").[22]

In contradistinction, former Alaska Governor and Vice-Presidential candidate Sarah Palin was blamed for using a "telescopic scope" metaphor of a "bullseye" on an election map of opposition Congressional districts. Jared Lee Loughner went so far as to claim that such a metaphor posited by Palin proximately caused/incited a mass shooting. As to the use of this same metaphor of the "bullseye," President Joe Biden declaimed: "I have one job, and that's to beat Donald Trump. I'm absolutely certain I'm the best person to be able to do that. So, we're done talking about the debate, it's time to put Trump in a bullseye." The legal implications of potentially inflammatory political rhetoric must be evaluated consistently regardless of the speaker's political affiliation. Consider as well, Biden's former "beat-up" violent rhetoric: "If we were in high school, I'd take him behind the gym and beat the hell out of him." "The press always asks me, 'Don't I wish I were debating him?' No,

22. Hanson, V. D. (2024, July 15). *Assassination porn and the sickness on the left.* Jewish News Syndicate. https://www.jns.org/assassination-porn-and-the-sickness-on-the-left/.

I wish we were in high school—I could take him behind the gym. That's what I wish."[23]

Sociopathic rhetoric proliferates as Hanson opines. *The New Republic* defiantly explained their Hitler-Trump cover photo this way: "Today, we at *The New Republic* think we can spend this election year in one of two ways. We can spend it debating whether Trump meets the nine or 17 points that define fascism. Or we can spend it saying, 'He's damn close enough, and we'd better fight.'" Hanson identifies MSNBC Joy Reid alleging Trump is a Hitlerian dictator: "Then let me know who I got to vote for to keep Hitler out of the White House." Hanson also observes Rachel Maddow on MSNBC "bloviating about studying Hitler to understand Trump." Words lead to ideas, and ideas indeed have consequences.

The Violence Prevention Research Program at the University of California, Davis, published that nearly fourteen percent of those surveyed "strongly agreed" that there would be civil war in the United States in the next few years. Nearly eight percent of respondents to the study said they believed there would be a situation in the next few years where "political violence would be justified" and were intending to arm themselves.[24]

23. Hanson, V. D. (2024, July 15). *Assassination porn and the sickness on the left*. Jewish News Syndicate. https://www.jns.org/assassination-porn-and-the-sickness-on-the-left/.

24. Feuer, A. *The New York Times.*

FACTUAL ANALYSIS

"The first rule of assassination—assassinate the assassins!" quipped Captain James Tiberius Kirk.[1] The generation that sprouted in the 1960s became versed in this aphorism, having witnessed the assassination of the assassins of both Robert "Jack" Fitzgerald Kennedy and Robert "Bobby" Kennedy. Questions linger from these tragedies from a generation and a half ago, as questions, like swords of Damocles, hover, lingering over the gaping black holes in the alleged fact pattern of the recent failed assassination attempt.

Rushing to baseless, unfounded judgment is folly.[2] To adjudge a matter before acquiring all the evidence is "folly and shame."[3] So the Hebrew Bible warns of rushing to a premature, uninformed judgment:

מֵשִׁיב דָּבָר בְּטֶרֶם יִשְׁמָע
אִוֶּלֶת הִיא־לוֹ וּכְלִמָּה׃[4]

---

1. † In the treatment of "Factual Analysis," footnotes conform to the *Publication Manual of the American Psychological Association* (7th ed. 2020), except that theological references follow the *SBL Handbook of Style* (2nd ed. 2014), of the Society of Biblical Literature.

Captain James Tiberius Kirk, in *Star Trek VI*. Meyer, N. (Director). (1991). *Star Trek VI: The Undiscovered Country* [Film]. Paramount Pictures.

2. Steven E. Runge and Joshua R. Westbury, eds., *The Lexham Discourse Hebrew Bible* (Bellingham, WA: Lexham Press, 2012–2014), Prov. 18:13.

3. Prov. 18:13.

4. Steven E. Runge and Joshua R. Westbury, eds., *The Lexham Discourse Hebrew Bible* (Bellingham, WA: Lexham Press, 2012–2014), Prov. 18:13.

Literally, "the one returning/rendering [a conclusion/verdict/judgment] before hearing [all, the entirety, the whole] of a matter—it is folly to him, and shame to him!"[5]

An incomplete evidentiary base leads to errors in judgment. The entirety of the evidence is the base of thorough, accurate, and complete judgment.

The following segments are versions of the factual history of the fateful event as per key major news agencies:

Factual Chronology—Al Jazeera's Version of Factual Timeline

6:02 p.m.—Trump takes the stage and waves to crowd

6:11 p.m.—As Trump points to a chart on immigration, gunfire is heard and Trump grabs his right ear. Secret Service agents run to the stage as more shots are fired. A man in the crowd is killed and two are critically injured.

6:12 p.m.—Secret Service agents try to get Trump off the stage. He pauses to get his shoes, then raises his fist in the air and says "Fight," as the crowd cheers and chants "USA." Trump raises his fist again as he is pushed into an SUV and taken to Butler Memorial Hospital, about 11 miles away.

6:42 p.m.—The Secret Service issues a statement saying Trump is safe after "an incident" at the rally.

8:13 p.m.—President Joe Biden condemns the attack during a televised speech.

8:42 p.m.—Trump posts about the incident on Truth Social: "I was shot with a bullet that pierced the upper part of my right ear. I knew immediately that something was wrong in that I heard a whizzing sound, shots, and immediately felt the bullet ripping through the skin."

---

5. Author's translation of Proverbs 18.13:
מֵשִׁיב דָּבָר בְּטֶרֶם יִשְׁמָע אִוֶּלֶת הִיא־לֹו וּכְלִמָּה:
The Lexham Hebrew Bible (Bellingham, WA: Lexham Press, 2012), Pr 18:13.

1:34 a.m.—The FBI formally calls the attack on Trump an "assassination attempt."[6]

Factual Chronology—USA TODAY's Version of Factual Timeline

6:03 p.m.—Trump takes the stage to Lee Greenwood's "God Bless the USA" and waves to the crowd.

6:05 p.m.— Trump starts speaking.

6:11 p.m.—Multiple shots are heard as Trump grabs his ear and drops to the ground.

6:12 p.m.—Secret Service agents escort Trump into a vehicle as he gives a thumbs up.

6:42 p.m.—The Secret Service issues a statement that "an incident" took place at the rally and that Trump "is safe.[7]

7:49 p.m.—Secret Service Spokesman Anthony Guglielmi releases a statement saying agents killed the shooter and that one spectator was killed by the gunman and two were seriously injured.

8:42 p.m. —Trump posted on Truth Social: "It is incredible that such an act can take place in our Country. Nothing is known at this time about the shooter, who is now dead. I was shot with a bullet that pierced the upper part of my right ear. I knew immediately that something was wrong in that I heard a whizzing sound, shots, and immediately felt the bullet ripping through the skin. Much bleeding took place, so I realized then what was happening. GOD BLESS AMERICA!"

9:33 p.m.—The FBI Pittsburgh announces it would be the lead agency investigating the shooting.

---

6. Al Jazeera Staff. (2024, July 14). *Donald Trump rally shooting: Minute-by-minute timeline of what happened*. Al Jazeera. See https://www.aljazeera.com/news/2024/7/14/donald-trump-rally-shooting-minute-by-minute-timeline-of-what-happened.

7. Anthony Guglielmi @SecretSvcSpox.

11:52 p.m.— Kevin Rojek, special agent in charge of the Pittsburgh FBI office, calls the shooting an attempted assassination.[8]

Factual Chronology—The Washington Post's Version of Factual Timeline

1:00 p.m.—Thousands start arriving for the rally throughout the afternoon.

6:03 p.m. —Trump arrives an hour later than announced.

6:05 p.m.—Trump starts off pointing out the size of the crowd.

6:10 p.m.—Trump turns to the right to comment on a chart on immigration.

6:12 p.m.—The first of several shots is fired, and Trump grabs his right ear. He ducks behind the lectern as a second shot is heard. Secret Service agents yell at him to get down and jump on top of him. A spectator is killed and two others critically wounded by gunfire. A sniper kills the gunman on the roof of an office building next to the fairgrounds. Trump stands, raises his fist and shouts "Fight! Fight!" to the crowd.

6:13 p.m.—Trump continues pumping his fist as agents escort him into a black SUV and drive away.

8:42 p.m.—Trump posts on Truth Social that a bullet pierced the upper part of his right ear: "I knew immediately that something was wrong in that I heard a whizzing sound, shots, and immediately felt the bullet ripping through my skin. Much bleeding took place, so I realized then what was happening."[9]

8. Natalie Neysa Alund is a senior reporter for *USA TODAY*. She can be reached at nalund@usatoday.com and followed on X at @nataliealund.

9. Derek Hawkins; Updated July 14, 2024, at 9:56 a.m. EDT | Published July 14, 2024, at 1:41 a.m. EDT. Compare *Ranking Member Thompson introduces legislation to ensure no Secret Service protection for convicted felons sentenced to prison*, House Committee on Homeland Security – Democrats (2024, April 19). Retrieved July 16, 2025, from https://democrats-homeland.house.gov/news/

Factual Chronology—The Telegraph's Version of Factual Timeline

17:00: Trump is scheduled to appear

18:03: Lee Hazelwood's "God Bless the USA" plays as Trump takes the stage

18:11: Shots ring out

18:12: Surrounded by Secret Service agents, blood streaming down his face, Trump raises his fist and appears to cries out "Fight."

18:14: Trump's motorcade departs with the president

18:42: Secret Service confirms Trump is safe

19:03: Trump's campaign announces he is "fine."

Factual History—World Response According to The New York Times

Here's what some major leaders had to say.[10]

Hungary—"My thoughts and prayers are with President Donald Trump in these dark hours," Prime Minister Viktor Orban wrote on social media. Mr. Orban, a longtime Trump supporter, met with the former president at his Mar-a-Lago residence in Florida two days before the rally in Pennsylvania.

Israel—Prime Minister Benjamin Netanyahu, another close Trump ally, offered his prayers, adding that he was "shocked."

Mexico—President Andrés Manuel López Obrador, whom Mr. Trump has called a leader "I like and respect,"

---

legislation/ranking-member-thompson-introduces-legislation-to-ensure-no-secret-service-protection-for-convicted-felons-sentenced-to-prison.

10. Courtesy of *New York Times*, Keith Bradsher, Amy Chang Chien, Chris Cameron, Choe Sand-Hun, Matina Stevis-Gridneff, Marc, Santora, Motoko Rich, and Anupreeta Das.

took to social media to call the violence "irrational and inhumane."

Ecuador—President Daniel Noboa called the attack "unacceptable," adding that the shooting was "a critical example of what we are exposed to every day." Last year, an Ecuadorean presidential candidate, Fernando Villavicencio, was killed in Quito by gunmen on motorcycles.

Argentina—President Javier Milei, who has long praised the leadership of Mr. Trump, was active on social media late into the evening sharing dozens of posts in support of the former president. In his own post, Mr. Milei expressed "all my support and solidarity to President and candidate Donald Trump, victim of a cowardly assassination attempt."

Italy—"I am following with apprehension the updates from Pennsylvania, where the 45th President of the United States Donald Trump was shot during a rally," Prime Minister Georgia Meloni wrote. A conservative leader with deep ties to the American right, she added that she hoped that "the next few months of the electoral campaign will see dialogue and responsibility prevail over hatred and violence."

India—Prime Minister Narendra Modi, in a post from his official account on X, said he was "deeply concerned by the attack on my friend, former President Donald Trump," adding, "Our thoughts and prayers are with the family of the deceased, those injured and the American people."

China—The Ministry of Foreign Affairs issued a short statement: "China is concerned about the shooting of former President Trump. President Xi Jinping has conveyed his sympathies to former President Trump."

Canada—Prime Minister Justin Trudeau, who often sparred over policy disagreements with Mr. Trump when he was in office, said in a social media post that he was "sickened" to learn of the shooting. "It cannot be overstated—political violence is never acceptable."

Ukraine—President Volodymyr Zelensky, whose relationship with Mr. Trump got off to an awkward start after the 2019 phone call that led to then-President Trump's first impeachment, declared himself "appalled" and said, "Never should violence prevail," adding, "I wish America emerges stronger from this."

Britain—Prime Minister Keir Starmer, who assumed his role a little over a week ago, said in a statement that he was "appalled" by the shooting, adding, "Political violence in any form has no place in our societies, and my thoughts are with all the victims of this attack."

Japan—Prime Minister Fumio Kishida said in a social media post that "we must stand firm against violence that challenges democracy." Shinzo Abe, a former Japanese prime minister, was fatally shot while speaking at a political event in July 2022.

France—President Emmanuel Macron wrote on social media: "It is a tragedy for our democracies. France shares the shock and indignation of the American people."

South Korea—Posting on X, President Yoon Suk Yeol wrote, "I am appalled by the hideous act of political violence." He added, "The people of Korea stand in solidarity with the people of America."[11]

Current Theorizations—What Went Wrong? Did the US Secret Service Fail? If So, in Mere Negligence, Wanton Negligence, or Willful Negligence?

Oliver Alexander, an open-source intelligence (OSINT) analyst, exclaimed, "I am amazed they did not see the shooter crawling into position for his shots a mere 430 ft away." Further, he "noted that one law enforcement sniper stationed in the area was facing in the direction of the shooter" and "that the secret service rooftop

---

11. Doug Mills and *New York Times*, by Keith Bradsher and Amy Chang Chien. Reporting contributed by Chris Cameron, Choe SandHun, Matina StevisGridneff, Marc Santora, Motoko Rich, and Anupreeta Das.

was on a higher level than the shooter's rooftop—which in principle means they ought to have spotted him easily."[12]

Nicholas Irving, former U.S. special operations sniper dubbed the "Reaper," was incredulous that a "guy w/ a rifle got within 152+ yards from a presidential nominee, unseen, and got shots off . . . . We provided better diplomatic security when I was w/ Triple Canopy [a private security firm] as a contractor. Who TF is in charge of the Secret Service? . . . No [eyes] on a firing position that close? Sketch."[13]

Problematic is the alleged/purported post of Jonathan Willis, an alleged U.S. Secret Service Sniper on Station. The post alleges he, on station as a counter-sniper, was ordered not to engage for approximately three to four minutes. Questions abound, if authentic. Why not allow him to engage with immediacy, due to the urgency of the visible threat? What is the origin of this blurb? Is he still employed by the USSS? What evidence do we have this claim is true? *USA TODAY* was earnest to report the Secret Service's denial.[14] "But no one named Jonathan Willis was involved with that team. Nate Herring, a Secret Service spokesperson, told Reuters that there is no employee with that name at the agency and described the claim as false. *USA TODAY* contacted the Secret Service for comment, but the agency did not respond to the request."[15] Reuters reported the same, that the claim was not authentic.[16]

12. Rozina Sabur, Deputy U.S. Editor, *The Daily Telegraph.* Follow her on X @ RozinaSabur.

13. Rozina Sabur, Deputy U.S. Editor, *The Daily Telegraph.* Follow her on X @ RozinaSabur.

14. USA TODAY. (2024, July 23). *Fact check: No evidence supports claim that a Secret Service sniper named Jonathan Willis prevented an assassination attempt on Trump.* Retrieved July 16, 2025, from https://www.usatoday.com/story/ news/factcheck/2024/07/23/jonathan-willis-secret-service-sniper-fact-check/ 74493857007/.

15. Edwards, J. (2024, July 23). *Jonathan Willis Secret Service sniper? USA Today.* https://www.usatoday.com/story/news/factcheck/2024/07/23/jonathan-willis-secret-service-sniper-fact-check/.

16. Khan, S. (2024, July 18). *"Jonathan Willis" is not a Secret Service employee, says spokesperson. Reuters.* https://www.reuters.com/fact-check/jonathan-willis-is

Since the aftershock of the Lee Harvey Oswald syndrome, the "who done it" theories abound. Was there a conspiracy? Was Crooks a patsy? Did he act alone? Questions remain how Crooks actually got to the scenario. Was it in a white van that was parked not far from the shooting origination that mysteriously moved off the press radar screen a mere day or two after the event? As Billy Thoma, one of the neighbors near the scenario, told Fox News, he got home a little before 5 p.m., saw a van with an Arizona plate parked on the street, "and didn't think much of it."[17] When one of the cops opened the van door, "everyone jumped back," Thoma said.

He didn't know why, but he certainly was fearful there could be a bomb aboard. It put him a little on edge, he said. On July 18, Fox reported that "law enforcement combed through a white van believed to have been used by Thomas Matthew Crooks," the gunman who shot at Trump.[18] "Officers found explosives, including an improvised explosive device, inside the van, sources confirmed to Fox News."[19] "The sources could not say how many explosives or what kind but emphasized that more than one was found. There were also bomb-making materials found inside Crooks' house, the sources told Fox News."[20] The mysterious "white van" with

-not-secret-service-employee-says-spokesperson-2024–07–18/.,

17. Boas, P. (2024, July 26). *The mystery of a white van that disappeared after the Trump shooting begs the question: Must Arizona be connected to everything that is infamous? AZCentral.* https://www.azcentral.com/story/opinion/op-ed/philboas/2024/07/26/trump-shooting-white-van-arizona-plates-conspiracy/.

18. Boas, P. (2024, July 26). *The mystery of a white van that disappeared after the Trump shooting begs the question: Must Arizona be connected to everything that is infamous? AZCentral.* https://www.azcentral.com/story/opinion/op-ed/philboas/2024/07/26/trump-shooting-white-van-arizona-plates-conspiracy/.

19. Boas, P. (2024, July 26). *Opinion: The mystery of a white van that disappeared after the Trump shooting begs the question: Must Arizona be connected to everything that is infamous? AZ Central.* Retrieved July 16, 2025, from https://www.azcentral.com/story/opinion/op-ed/philboas/2024/07/26/trump-shooting-white-van-arizona-plates-conspiracy/74561929007/.

20. Boas, P. (2024, July 26). *Opinion: The mystery of a white van that disappeared after the Trump shooting begs the question: Must Arizona be connected to everything that is infamous? AZ Central.* Retrieved July 16, 2025, from https://

Arizona plates has not appeared on the press's radar screen since then—most mysteriously. And what of the owner of the van? Did Crooks arrive by bicycle, silver sedan, or by the white van—or did he arrive, leave and return? Valid questions abound—unanswered.

Then there is the question of the Secret Service and one's political opponents. Given the tragic history of the Kennedys, why in the world did the Biden administration not insist that third-party candidate Robert Kennedy Jr. be accorded Secret Service protection? Because his candidacy was felt to be disadvantageous to Biden? And why just this April would the former head of the January 6th Committee Rep. Bennie Thompson (D-Miss.) introduce legislation ridiculously entitled, "Denying Infinite Security and Government Resources Allocated Toward Convicted and Extremely Dishonorable (DISGRACED) Former Protectees Act"[21] to strip away Secret Service protection for former President Trump and by this April current leading presidential candidate?[22]

Some Have Alleged That the Entire Scene Was Orchestrated and Choreographed into a "Fake" Publicity Stunt

One theorization is that the assassination was "staged" in order to gain political points, so that a Presidential candidate would appear to be a martyr, or even resurrected. Arguments proceed as follows,

---

www.azcentral.com/story/opinion/op-ed/philboas/2024/07/26/trump-shooting-white-van-arizona-plates-conspiracy/74561929007/.

21. House Committee on Homeland Security – Democrats. (2024, April 19). *Ranking Member Thompson introduces legislation to ensure no Secret Service protection for convicted felons sentenced to prison.* Retrieved July 16, 2025, from https://democrats-homeland.house.gov/news/legislation/ranking-member-thompson-introduces-legislation-to-ensure-no-secret-service-protection-for-convicted-felons-sentenced-to-prison.

22. The Clarion Ledger. (2024, April 21). *Trump Secret Service protection could be removed under Rep. Bennie Thompson legislation. Clarion Ledger.* Retrieved July 16, 2025, from https://www.clarionledger.com/story/news/2024/04/21/trump-secret-service-protection-could-be-removed-under-rep-bennie-thompson-legislation/73406474007/.

pro and con. Arguments for the staged, "faked" assassination attempt to "make political hay" are as follows:

(1)Political Motivation

Conspiracy theorists allege that the presidential candidate, to achieve resurrected martyr status, actually planned a staged fake assassination, and even though one man was murdered, the murder was justified as the needs of the many outweigh the needs of the few. Others theorize that the "patsy" assassin was first a registered Republican (although he supported Democrat causes) "set up" to suggest the political base is inherently violent,

(2)Early Contradictory Reports

Early indistinct reports regarding sustained injuries, lapse in law enforcement, and timing questions fomented doubt as to the actuality. Odd angles and blocked visuals also fueled denial. Some falsely identified the killer, and others mistook his body.[23] One viral post alleged that there was, for instance, another victim by a second shooter, likely from the mysterious "white van," but no verification has been confirmed.[24] Democrat fact checkers, including PolitiFact, CBS, Reuters, Snopes, and Media Matters, as well as major Democrat-leaning newspapers, found no objective evidence to support staging theorizations.

23. Sanders, K. (2024, July 15). *When Donald Trump was shot, the internet unleashed wild conspiracy theories.* PolitiFact. Retrieved July 18, 2025, from https://www.politifact.com/article/2024/jul/15/when-donald-trump-was-shot-the-internet-unleashed/?utm_source=chatgpt.com.

24. Reuters. (2024, August 5). *Man in clip not hit by bullet at Trump rally, not proof of a second shooter.* Reuters. Retrieved July 18, 2025 from https://www.reuters.com/fact-check/man-clip-not-hit-by-bullet-trump-rally-not-proof-second-shooter-2024-08-05/

(3) Supposed Historical Examples of Falsification

Conspiracy theorists who surmise that the tragedy of 9/11 was computer-generated to create a pretext to go to war in the Middle East, and that the mRNA vaccine is "poison" to kill Westerners, were more prone to falsely theorize the tragic event via distorted paranoia. In the stress and strain of the vivid assassination attempt, "unleashed wild conspiracy theories" erupted like an explosive volcano.[25] Past incidents of false-flag operations for political theater condition some conspiracy theorists to surmise positions of power-stage crises for political gain. Dorman B. Eaton, for instance, in his influential 1881 work *The "Spoils" System and Civil Service Reform in the Custom-House and Post-Office at New York*, declaims against power elites who manipulate public perception for power, prestige, and position.[26] Aldous Huxley, in his famous 1958 interview with Mike Wallace, warned of political packaging of candidates that may as well be a mirage.[27]

(4) Lapses and Negligence by Law Enforcement

The unhindered climbing onto the roof by the assassin, with his weapon manifest, led some to conclude that the attempt was permitted, or even planned. Secret Service and Congressional investigations found severe, blatant negligence, demonstrating that weakness was not conspiracy.[28]

25. Sanders, K. (2024, July 15). *When Donald Trump was shot, the internet unleashed wild conspiracy theories.* PolitiFact. Retrieved July 18, 2025, from https://www.politifact.com/article/2024/jul/15/when-donald-trump-was-shot-the-internet-unleashed/?utm_source=chatgpt.com.

26. Eaton, D. B. (1881). *The "spoils" system and civil service reform in the CustomHouse and PostOffice at New York.* New York: G. P. Putnam's Sons.

27. Wallace, M. (Interviewer), & Huxley, A. (1958, May 18). *The Mike Wallace Interview: Aldous Huxley [Television broadcast].* ABC-TV. Retrieved from https://www.youtube.com/watch?v=1ePNGaom3XA (en.wikipedia.org+15youtube.com+15huxleyarchive.org+15).

28. OpenAI. (2025, July 18). *ChatGPT conversation: 687947192118800aae9d2 ee7c4e9f5do* [AI-generated text]. ChatGPT. Retrieved July 18, 2025, from https://chatgpt.com/c/68794719-2118-800a-ae9d-2ee7c4e9f5do.

Arguments Against the "Faked/Staged" Theory—Contra Evidence and Considerations

(1) Law Enforcement Investigations with Commensurate Evidence

Law enforcement on the scene, local police, Secret Service, and FBI confirmed an actual shooting with ballistic evidence. Photographic, videographic, and medical reports verified Trump's ear injury and the death of a bystander. Photograph and videographic evidence discount and deny a "blood pill" supposedly bit and spewed for a faked dramatic theatrical stunt.

(2) Sight and Sound Witness Testimonials

Sight and sound eyewitnesses on the scene, including journalists and rally attendees, corroborate the fact pattern of the event, with matching accounts of gunfire. Videographic evidence from multiple angles corroborates the sequence of events.

(3) Implausibility, Even Impossibility, of Large-Scale Deception

Faking, staging, rigging, and orchestrating a dramatized assassination attempt of the scale in Butler would require coordination across agencies, media, witnesses and bystanders—a near-impossible Herculean task. The likely risk of exposure by non-compliant whistleblowers, scrupulous truth-tellers, and forensic analysts render it highly unlikely, if not outrightly untenable.

(4) Angry, Activist, Propagandistic Anti-Trump Circles Habitually Discredit and Defame

Some more-motivated activists, particularly in leftist, anarchist, or alleged "anti-fascist" (antifa) circles, view Trump as a chronic, pathological liar and Hitlerian authoritarian figure. Orwellian hate leads to blanket skepticism about his narratives. However, they typically focus on his policies/rhetoric rather than denying violent events like the assassination attempt. The proverbial Orwellian "Two Minutes" daily hate ritual would require true citizens to express a hate-rage against the real or imagined enemy of the state, Emmanual Goldstein. Hate spews from such rage whether facts support or disprove allegations. The hate-entities diminish, depreciate, degrade, deprecate, demode, discredit, deny, debilitate, destroy, and defame the hate-object. Any positive event such a psychology is apt to deny.

(5) Tankie, Marxist-Leninist, and Neo-Communist Groups

Extreme authoritarian leftists—"tankie," Marxist-Leninist, and neo-Communist factions— attempt to discredit all Western, especially American, institutions—alleging, for instance, "your elections are magic" and "your government is a Uniparty medical slave state, requiring you be poisoned with mRNA." Russian, Chinese, and Jihadist propaganda denigrates Western institutions as a sham. Stalin and Putin "tankies"—apologists who defend both Stalin and Putin rolling, respectively, tanks into Budapest, Prague, and the Donbas, as well as attempting armored incursion into Kharkiv and Kyiv—undermine confidence in Western institutions. All Western political events are "bourgeoisie propaganda." Niche trolls allege such events as Apollo landing on the moon, 9/11 Islamist terrorism, and the attempted assassination of July 13, 2024, are "bourgeoisie propaganda." Smears without evidence are Faustian and Machiavellian. Leftist contrarian figures such as Chris Hedges or Caitlin Johnstone frame Trump as a "controlled opposition" puppet, alleging his populist façade of rooting out the elitist-globalist-run "Deep State" actually channels resistance back into an establishment party that is part of a "Uniparty" megalith controlled by plutocrats. In a mindset of a plutocratic oligarchy, appearances may be orchestrated to manipulate the masses. Media manipulation is "opium of the people" to make the masses controllable. Without dispositive evidence, smears of the contrarian far left lack teeth—are "bark with no bite." The central motto and meme "everything from Trump, about Trump, for Trump, around Trump, through Trump, of Trump is a lie" is a hyperbolic sentiment found in extremist far left and anti-Trump circles, though it rarely extends to outrageous claims that the attempted assassination was an orchestrated, staged political campaign stunt that even went so far as to murder an innocent bystander.

(6) Key Democrat Fact Checks and Their Findings

Significant Democrat fact checkers have confirmed the attempted assassination was real. Snopes, for instance, confirmed the "stage publicity campaign stunt" was "false" because of law-enforcement examination, bullet trajectories, and eyewitness accounts, as well as medical reports confirming the injuries. Further, orchestrating such a complex, far-reaching ruse without leaks is virtually impossible. Media Matters also underscored how the claim originated from "far-right conspiracy circles" and spread via disinformation networks. Media Matters opined that no credible evidence supports the "faked" staged narrative. Further, the AP News Fact Check discounted and denied the theory by citing video evidence of the shooting, statements from Secret Service and local law enforcement, and lack of motive for such an elaborate hoax. Multiple Democrat independent fact checkers reached the same conclusion. Further, the major Democrat-leaning news networks CBS, ABC, NBC, NPR, MSNBC,[29] CNN, New York Times, and Washington Post confirm the assassination attempt was real—and would certainly have exploited it for enormous political hay if it was a campaign ruse.

Although MSNBC, as committed to Democrat narratives as it is, as a whole never endorsed the "faked/staged" conspiracy

---

29. Gerasimov, V. (2013, February). The value of science is in the foresight: New challenges demand rethinking the forms and methods of carrying out combat operations (R. Coalson, Trans.). *Military-Industrial Courier*. (Original work published in Russian).

theory, Joy Reid, then of MSNBC, on July 18, 2024, in an individual broadcast aired on Twitter/X, did allege that Donald Trump was never hit by a bullet, mistaking the healing of the ear injury as if she has medical training, as well as observing that law enforcement allowed Crooks to climb onto the roof with a weapon, surmising a conspiracy. In immediate response/reaction was Charlie Kirk, who on Twitter/X demanded MSNBC fire Joy Reid. Later, on February 25, 2025, MSNBC fired Joy Reid for undisclosed reason(s).

While conspiracy theories thrive on institutional distrust and psychological paranoia, the plethora of evidence supports the narrative that the July 13, 2024, assassination was real. The left tends to associate "fake event" theories with right-wing movements, such as QAnon and Sandy Hook denialism, even though the left maintained the most extensive of conspiracy theories, debunked by the Democrat lawyers under Bob Mueller producing the exonerating Mueller report—the mythological, libelous Russian collusion *"große Lüge,"* Goebbels' term for "big lie." The stubborn persistence of such conspiratorial claims derives from a deep-rooted political skepticism of government narratives.

While some on the left argue Trump's entire persona is built on deception, very few extend the perceptual bias and prejudice to deny the actual physical reality of the assassination attempt. The "faked" narrative remains overwhelmingly among impaired, imbalanced, and outrageous extremists, or actual deliberate propagandists, domestic and foreign.
Credible evidence is replete that the Russian propaganda machine fueled дезинформация (*dezinformatsiya*) alleging that the assassination attempt on July 13, 2024, was a staged false flag. Russia Times (RT) and Sputnik, Russian state propaganda organs, fomented false/fraudulent narratives—the Biden administration/Deep State attempted the assassination, Ukrainian intelligence orchestrated the attempt to prevent a reduction in arms shipments, or MAGA activists faked the event to present Trump as a resurrected martyr. Kremlin propagandists cast the event as evidence of the collapse of American democracy. Kremlin press secretary

Dmitry Peskov implied Biden himself "put Trump in danger" with rhetoric to "stop" him. A spawn/offshoot of Prigozhin's Internet Research Agency, *Storm-1516,* as well as the Doppelganger site, deployed comments utilizing their thousands of aliases to spread the conspiracy narrative that the assassination was a publicity stunt. One particular doctored video of the Republican National Convention, for instance, falsely presented the wound on the left ear, rather than the actual injury on the right ear. Even Democrat or pro-Democrat news agencies, such as Reuters and the Associated Press (AP), exposed the misrepresentation in fact-checking.[30] Scott Carney, in his "The Truth Behind Trump's Assassination" in *The Atlantic,* points out that Crooks was removed from his high-school rifle team because his inaccuracy was deemed a danger to his classmates. Carney opines, to paraphrase, "Why would an inaccurate shooter be hired to fire a near miss?" Carney also points out, to paraphrase: "Trump was exempted from military service because of 'bone spurs' and has never been in combat. Would he be willing to risk a near miss from an amateur?"[31] Extremist conspiracy theorists even allege the photographers were moved into place to acquire an optimal photo shoot to help the Trump campaign—forty-nine (49) seconds transpired between the shot that wounded and the taking of the iconic triumphant bloody fist pump photo. The Pulitzer and Edward R. Murrow award-winning Evan Vucci of The Associated Press (AP) took the iconic photo, yet later sued the Trump Administration for disallowing him access to the White House. Carney further posits, to paraphrase, "Would Vucci be part of a conspiracy and later sue the orchestrators of the conspiracy?"[32] Further, some opine the ear healed too quickly—an

30. Gerasimov, V. (2013, February). The value of science is in the foresight: New challenges demand rethinking the forms and methods of carrying out combat operations (R. Coalson, Trans.). *Military-Industrial Courier.* (Original work published in Russian).

31. Scott Carney. (2024, May 10). *The truth behind Trump's assassination.* The Atlantic. https://www.theatlantic.com/article-url. Carney, S. (2025, July 22). The truth behind Trump's assassination [Video]. YouTube. https://www.youtube.com/watch?v=KgeNlepzoiw.

32. Scott Carney. (2024, May 10). *The truth behind Trump's assassination.* The

ear cartilage graze with prompt medical treatment would include cleaning, suturing, possible steroid injections, and plastic surgery if necessary. And of course, such a candidate would have the best makeup artists money can buy.

The standard "echo chamber" propaganda tactic—fraudulent report, fake websites, false aliases—expand the scope of influence worldwide in a matter of seconds, as per General Valery Gerasimov's white paper circulated in 2013 as Chief of the Russian General Staff. The Russian white paper, a widely discussed military doctrine, was later coined as "Fifth Generation Hybrid Warfare." The "hybrid" warfare doctrine of General Valery (Vasilyevich) Gerasimov—the then–Chief of the Russian General Staff—was popularized in article titled *"The Value of Science Is in the Foresight: New Challenges Demand Rethinking the Forms and Methods of Carrying Out Combat Operations,"* and further evolved in subsequent Kremlin publications. In sum, the Russian Fifth General Hybrid Warfare doctrine is that for every Russian soldier wielding an AK-47 or AKM, there must be approximately four backing that soldier up on the internet, proclaiming the armed soldier a hero, and their opposition demonic. Gerasimov advocates for wars to be won by internet propaganda, as well as by arms, on the model of the pro-North Vietnamese propagandists. First-generation warfare: Cain kills Abel hand to hand; second-generation warfare: organized armies kill organized armies "up close and personal" pre-gunpowder; third-generation warfare: post-gunpowder armed forces kill weaker armed forces; fourth-generation warfare: nuclear weapons make destruction so devastating to the point of mutual assured destruction; fifth-generation warfare: worldwide propaganda shifts public opinion so that arms and propaganda work in conjunction to expand the "Русский мир," The Russian World.

Mark Galeotti coined the series of Kremlin publications as the "Gerasimov Doctrine"—a synchronization of strategic operations, intertwining disinformation warfare, cyber-attacks/sabotage,

Atlantic. https://www.theatlantic.com/article-url. Carney, S. (2025, July 22). The truth behind Trump's assassination [Video]. YouTube. https://www.youtube.com/watch?v=KgeNlepzoiw.

political lobbying, and election interference, as well as full-blown kinetic invasions, as in the attack on Ukraine in February 2022. Asymmetric propaganda intrusions exert influence alongside threats, if not deployments, of military force. Opponents are destabilized, diminished, and disrupted by technologically advanced tools such as bots, in non-kinetic force, with kinetic force versatile enough to adapt to interior domestic terrorism, border skirmishes, and escalation to "tankie" full-blown invasion. Asymmetrical, non-linear, non-kinetic means and methods may precede, assist, coordinate, and promote potential and actual kinetic deployments of lethal force.

Traditional distinctions between "state of war" and "peace in our time" are washed away by the Gerasimov doctrine—no sharp line divides the two categories. Mother Russia is always in New Generation Hybrid Warfare, weakening actual and potential enemies, destabilizing opponents via covert operations, filling the internet waves with propaganda to create adherents, and ready for flexible, limited-scope deployments of forces. Phased, interspersed, hybrid expansions of power comprise the core of the Gerasimov doctrine.[33]

Finally, the idea that bystanders spotted a 20-year-old on a nearby roof with a gun, a mere 130 yards from Trump, and in vain warned police of his presence, is surreal.[34] Is it all that hard for the Secret Service to post a few agents on the tops of a few surrounding buildings closest to the dais, or at least coordinate with local law enforcement to do the same?[35] Is not a "no-brainer"? Whoever made the decisions concerning the proper Secret Service security details for presidential events should been immediately

33. Gerasimov, V. (2013, February). The value of science is in the foresight: New challenges demand rethinking the forms and methods of carrying out combat operations (R. Coalson, Trans.). *Military-Industrial Courier*. (Original work published in Russian).

34. Free Republic. Retrieved July 16, 2025, from https://www.freerepublic.com/focus/f-news/4251330/posts.

35. Free Republic. Retrieved July 16, 2025, from https://www.freerepublic.com/focus/f-news/4251330/posts.

fired,[36] not resign under Congressional pressure. Fortunately, the would-be assassin was an amateur. A professional would have hit his target.

Congress's Factual Analysis—Task Force Release September 25, 2024, Summary[37]

Regarding the colossal, multiple failures of July 13, 2024, on September 25, 2024, U.S. Senators Gary Peters (D-MI) and Rand Paul (R-KY), Chairman and Ranking Member of the Homeland Security and Governmental Affairs Committee (HSGAC), and Richard Blumenthal (D-CT) and Ron Johnson (R-WI), Chairman and Ranking Member of the Permanent Subcommittee on Investigations, released a bipartisan interim report on the U.S. Secret Service's (USSS) security planning, communications and coordination failures that contributed to the July 13 assassination attempt on former President Donald. J. Trump in Butler, Pennsylvania. The interim report's key findings of failures of the U.S. Secret Service include:

- **USSS failed to clearly define responsibilities for planning and security at the July 13 rally:** USSS personnel responsible for planning in advance of the July 13 rally denied that they were individually responsible for any planning or security failures and deflected blame. USSS Advance Leads told the Committee that planning and security decisions were made jointly, with no specific individual responsible for approval.[38]

---

36. Free Republic. Retrieved July 16, 2025, from https://www.freerepublic.com/focus/f-news/4251330/posts.

37. House Task Force on the Attempted Assassination of Donald J. Trump. (2024, October 21). *Interim staff report: Investigating the stunning security failures on July 13, 2024 in Butler, Pennsylvania* [PDF]. U.S. House of Representatives. Retrieved July 16, 2025, from https://taskforce.house.gov/sites/evo-subsites/july13taskforce.house.gov/files/evo-media-document/task-force-interim-staff-report-10.21.2024.pdf.

38. U.S. Senate Homeland Security and Governmental Affairs Committee. (2024, September 25). *Peters, Paul, Blumenthal, and Johnson release bipartisan*

- **USSS failed to ensure the AGR Building was effectively covered:** USSS identified the AGR building as a concern due to the line-of-sight from the roof to the stage but did not take steps to ensure sufficient security measures were in place. USSS knew that local snipers planned to set up inside the AGR building and USSS did not express objections or concerns about that placement. USSS personnel, including the USSS Counter Sniper Team Leader, did not enter the AGR building or go on the roof prior to the shooting. One USSS counter sniper team, whose responsibility included scanning the area around the AGR building for threats, had an obstructed view of the AGR roof.[39]

- **USSS failed to effectively coordinate with state and local law enforcement:** USSS did not give state or local partners any specific instructions for covering the AGR building, including the positioning of local snipers. USSS did not adequately consider state and local law enforcement operational plans. Communications at the July 13 rally were siloed and USSS did not ensure it could share information with local law enforcement partners in real time.[40]

report examining *U.S. Secret Service security failures and assassination attempt on former President Trump.* Retrieved July 16, 2025, from https://www.hsgac.senate.gov/media/dems/peters-paul-blumenthal-and-johnson-release-bipartisan-report -examining-u-s-secret-service-security-failures-and-assassination-attempt-on-former-president-trump/.

39. U.S. Senate Homeland Security and Governmental Affairs Committee. (2024, September 25). *Peters, Paul, Blumenthal, and Johnson release bipartisan report examining U.S. Secret Service security failures and assassination attempt on former President Trump.* Retrieved July 16, 2025, from https://www.hsgac.senate.gov/media/dems/peters-paul-blumenthal-and-johnson-release-bipartisan-report -examining-u-s-secret-service-security-failures-and-assassination-attempt-on-former-president-trump/.

40. U.S. Senate Homeland Security and Governmental Affairs Committee. (2024, September 25). *Peters, Paul, Blumenthal, and Johnson release bipartisan report examining U.S. Secret Service security failures and assassination attempt on former President Trump.* Retrieved July 16, 2025, from https://www.hsgac.senate.gov/media/dems/peters-paul-blumenthal-and-johnson-release-bipartisan-report -examining-u-s-secret-service-security-failures-and-assassination-attempt-on-former-president-trump/.

- **USSS failed to provide resources for the July 13 rally that could have enhanced security:** USSS denied specific requests for additional Counter Unmanned Aircraft Systems capabilities and a Counter Assault Team liaison. A USSS Counter Surveillance Unit—which could have helped patrol the outer perimeter that included the AGR building—was not requested by USSS Advance Leads.[41]

- **USSS failed to communicate information about the suspicious person to key personnel and failed to take action to ensure the safety of former President Trump:** At approximately 5:44 pm, USSS personnel were notified that local law enforcement observed a suspicious person with a rangefinder near the AGR building. By 5:52 pm, at least eight USSS personnel had been informed. Approximately two minutes before shots were fired, the USSS Security Room, located on the rally grounds, was told there was an individual on the roof of the AGR building. Shortly before shots were fired, a USSS counter sniper observed local officers running towards the AGR building with guns drawn.[42]

- **USSS's counter drone system experienced technical problems that left it inoperable for hours:** With no backup system, the USSS agent responsible for overseeing the C-UAS capabilities at the July 13 rally called a toll-free 888 tech support hotline "to start troubleshooting with the company,"

41. U.S. Senate Homeland Security and Governmental Affairs Committee. (2024, September 25). *Peters, Paul, Blumenthal, and Johnson release bipartisan report examining U.S. Secret Service security failures and assassination attempt on former President Trump*. Retrieved July 16, 2025, from https://www.hsgac.senate.gov/media/dems/peters-paul-blumenthal-and-johnson-release-bipartisan-report-examining-u-s-secret-service-security-failures-and-assassination-attempt-on-former-president-trump/.

42. U.S. Senate Homeland Security and Governmental Affairs Committee. (2024, September 25). *Peters, Paul, Blumenthal, and Johnson release bipartisan report examining U.S. Secret Service security failures and assassination attempt on former President Trump*. Retrieved July 16, 2025, from https://www.hsgac.senate.gov/media/dems/peters-paul-blumenthal-and-johnson-release-bipartisan-report-examining-u-s-secret-service-security-failures-and-assassination-attempt-on-former-president-trump/.

which took several hours. That agent had only three months of experience working with that equipment and lacked knowledge about it.[43]

- **Several USSS officials reported experiencing technical problems with their radios at the rally, and told the Committee such problems are common for USSS:** A USSS Hercules 1 counter sniper was offered a local radio on July 13 but said he did not have time to pick it up because he was occupied fixing technical problems with his USSS radio. In addition, at the Pittsburgh airport before the motorcade left for the rally, the USSS Special Agent in Charge (SAIC) of the Pittsburgh field office gave the Lead Agent his radio because the Lead Agent's radio was not working."[44]

Excerpts from the Task Force Report

"In a series of transcribed interviews conducted by Homeland Security and Governmental Affairs Committee (HSGAC) and the Permanent Subcommittee on Investigations, key USSS personnel responsible for planning, coordinating, communicating, and securing the Butler, PA rally on July 13, declined to acknowledge individual areas of responsibility for planning or security as having contributed to the failure to prevent the shooting that day, even

43. U.S. Senate Homeland Security and Governmental Affairs Committee. (2024, September 25). *Peters, Paul, Blumenthal, and Johnson release bipartisan report examining U.S. Secret Service security failures and assassination attempt on former President Trump.* Retrieved July 16, 2025, from https://www.hsgac.senate.gov/media/dems/peters-paul-blumenthal-and-johnson-release-bipartisan-report-examining-u-s-secret-service-security-failures-and-assassination-attempt-on-former-president-trump/.

44. U.S. Senate Homeland Security and Governmental Affairs Committee. (2024, September 25). *Peters, Paul, Blumenthal, and Johnson release bipartisan report examining U.S. Secret Service security failures and assassination attempt on former President Trump.* Retrieved July 16, 2025, from https://www.hsgac.senate.gov/media/dems/peters-paul-blumenthal-and-johnson-release-bipartisan-report-examining-u-s-secret-service-security-failures-and-assassination-attempt-on-former-president-trump/.

when as an agency, the USSS has acknowledged ultimate responsibility for the failure to prevent the former president of the United States from being shot."[45]

"As discussed at the conclusion of this interim report, key requests to FBI, DHS, ATF and USSS remain outstanding. The majority of documents provided by the USSS and DHS are heavily redacted. This has unnecessarily hindered the Committee's ability to carry out its constitutional authority to investigate and acquire information necessary to identify needed reforms. These overly burdensome redactions, including of communications related to the same individuals who the Committee interviewed, only served to delay the Committee's ability to conduct these interviews and carry out its investigation efficiently and effectively."[46]

". . . several USSS individuals responsible for planning and security for the July 13 rally provided contradictory or incomplete information, some of which ran counter to responses from state and local law enforcement officials and even other USSS personnel."[47]

45. U.S. Senate Homeland Security and Governmental Affairs Committee. (2024, October 21). *Examination of U.S. Secret Service planning and security failures related to the July 13, 2024 assassination attempt* [PDF]. Retrieved July 16, 2025, from https://www.hsgac.senate.gov/wp-content/uploads/USSS-HSGAC-Interim-Report.pdf.

46. U.S. House Task Force on the Attempted Assassination of Donald J. Trump. (2024, October 21). *Interim staff report: Investigating the stunning security failures on July 13, 2024, in Butler, Pennsylvania* [PDF]. Retrieved July 16, 2025, from https://taskforce.house.gov/sites/evo-subsites/july13taskforce.house.gov/files/evo-media-document/task-force-interim-staff-report-10.21.2024.pdf, p. 4.

47. U.S. House Task Force on the Attempted Assassination of Donald J. Trump. (2024, October 21). *Interim staff report: Investigating the stunning security failures on July 13, 2024, in Butler, Pennsylvania* [PDF]. Retrieved July 16, 2025, from https://taskforce.house.gov/sites/evo-subsites/july13taskforce.house.gov/files/evo-media-document/task-force-interim-staff-report-10.21.2024.pdf, pp. 4–5.

"USSS personnel responsible for planning in advance of the July 13 rally denied that they were individually responsible for planning or security failures and deflected blame."[48]

"USSS identified the AGR building as a concern due to the line-of-sight from the roof to the stage, but did not take steps to ensure sufficient security measures were in place. . . .
One USSS Counter Sniper team, whose responsibility included scanning the area around the AGR building for threats, had an obstructed view of the AGR roof."[49]

"Communications at the July 13 rally were siloed and USSS did not ensure it could share information with local law enforcement partners in real time."[50]

"USSS failed to provide resources for the July 13 rally that could have enhanced security. USSS denied specific requests for additional Counter Unmanned Aircraft Systems (C-UAS) capabilities and a Counter Assault Team liaison. . . . USSS failed to communicate information about the suspicious person to key personnel, and failed to take action to ensure the safety of former President Trump."[51]

48. U.S. House Task Force on the Attempted Assassination of Donald J. Trump. (2024, October 21). *Interim staff report: Investigating the stunning security failures on July 13, 2024, in Butler, Pennsylvania* [PDF]. Retrieved July 16, 2025, from https://taskforce.house.gov/sites/evo-subsites/july13taskforce.house.gov/files/evo-media-document/task-force-interim-staff-report-10.21.2024.pdf, p. 5.

49. U.S. House Task Force on the Attempted Assassination of Donald J. Trump. (2024, October 21). *Interim staff report: Investigating the stunning security failures on July 13, 2024, in Butler, Pennsylvania* [PDF]. Retrieved July 16, 2025, from https://taskforce.house.gov/sites/evo-subsites/july13taskforce.house.gov/files/evo-media-document/task-force-interim-staff-report-10.21.2024.pdf, p. 5.

50. U.S. House Task Force on the Attempted Assassination of Donald J. Trump. (2024, October 21). *Interim staff report: Investigating the stunning security failures on July 13, 2024, in Butler, Pennsylvania* [PDF]. Retrieved July 16, 2025, from https://taskforce.house.gov/sites/evo-subsites/july13taskforce.house.gov/files/evo-media-document/task-force-interim-staff-report-10.21.2024.pdf, p. 6.

51. U.S. House Task Force on the Attempted Assassination of Donald J. Trump. (2024, October 21). *Interim staff report: Investigating the stunning security failures on July 13, 2024, in Butler, Pennsylvania* [PDF]. Retrieved July 16, 2025,

"Shortly before shots were fired, a USSS counter sniper saw local law enforcement running toward the AGR building with their guns drawn, but he did not alert former President Trump's protective detail to remove him from the stage. The USSS counter sniper told the Committee that while seeing officers with their guns drawn 'elevated' the threat level, the thought to notify someone to get Trump off the stage 'did not cross [his] mind.'"

"USSS counter snipers—including the one who shot and killed Crooks—were sent to the rally in response to 'credible intelligence' of a threat. The July 13 rally was the first time a USSS counter sniper team was assigned to a protectee other than the President, Vice President, or a presidential candidate who had been formally nominated by his or her party. USSS provided the counter snipers in response to 'credible intelligence' of a threat. However, FBI has said that Crooks 'was not known to the FBI prior to' the assassination attempt."[52]

"A member of Butler ESU told the Committee that he notified USSS Advance Agents during a walkthrough on Thursday, July 11 that local law enforcement did not have the 'manpower' to lock down the AGR building. USSS Advance Agents interviewed by the Committee gave conflicting accounts and told the Committee that state and local law enforcement were responsible for covering the AGR building because it was in the outer perimeter. Prior to the July 13 rally, the USSS Lead Advance Agent, Counter Sniper Team Leader, and Site Counterpart did not go into the AGR building. None of the USSS Advance Agents shared planning documents with state or local law enforcement, or requested state or local

from https://taskforce.house.gov/sites/evo-subsites/july13taskforce.house.gov/files/evo-media-document/task-force-interim-staff-report-10.21.2024.pdf, p. 6.

52. U.S. House Task Force on the Attempted Assassination of Donald J. Trump. (2024, October 21). *Interim staff report: Investigating the stunning security failures on July 13, 2024, in Butler, Pennsylvania* [PDF]. Retrieved July 16, 2025, from https://taskforce.house.gov/sites/evo-subsites/july13taskforce.house.gov/files/evo-media-document/task-force-interim-staff-report-10.21.2024.pdf, p. 7.

operational plans—and those plans reveal no post-standers or patrol assigned to cover the AGR building or roof."[53]

"There were two separate communications centers at the July 13 rally—one run by USSS and one by local law enforcement. The posts were anywhere from 120 to 300 yards apart from each other and the primary means of communication between the posts was by cell phone. Local law enforcement and USSS operated on separate radio channels. All of the local channels were recorded on July 13, but USSS radio transmissions were not."[54]

"Several USSS officials reported experiencing technical problems with their radios at the rally, and told the Committee such problems are common for USSS. A USSS Hercules 1 counter sniper was offered a local radio on July 13 but said he did not have time to pick it up because he was occupied fixing technical problems with his USSS radio. In addition, at the Pittsburgh airport before the motorcade left for the rally, the USSS SAIC of the Pittsburgh Field Office gave the Lead Advance Agent his radio because the Lead Advance Agent's radio was not working. As a result, the SAIC did not have a working radio on him during his entire time at the July 13 rally. While he did not 'hold a post or a sector' and was 'not part of any protective formation,' he did claim that he was there to 'act more in a liaison capacity.' However, he did not have any means to communicate on the radio with his USSS counterparts."[55]

53. U.S. House Task Force on the Attempted Assassination of Donald J. Trump. (2024, October 21). *Interim staff report: Investigating the stunning security failures on July 13, 2024, in Butler, Pennsylvania* [PDF]. Retrieved July 16, 2025, from https://taskforce.house.gov/sites/evo-subsites/july13taskforce.house.gov/files/evo-media-document/task-force-interim-staff-report-10.21.2024.pdf, p. 7.

54. U.S. House Task Force on the Attempted Assassination of Donald J. Trump. (2024, October 21). *Interim staff report: Investigating the stunning security failures on July 13, 2024, in Butler, Pennsylvania* [PDF]. Retrieved July 16, 2025, from https://taskforce.house.gov/sites/evo-subsites/july13taskforce.house.gov/files/evo-media-document/task-force-interim-staff-report-10.21.2024.pdf, pp. 8–9.

55. U.S. House Task Force on the Attempted Assassination of Donald J. Trump. (2024, October 21). *Interim staff report: Investigating the stunning security failures on July 13, 2024, in Butler, Pennsylvania* [PDF]. Retrieved July 16, 2025,

At a Congressional Task Force hearing on September 26, 2024, Chairman Mike Kelly stated: "In the days leading up to the rally, it was not a single mistake that allowed Crooks to outmaneuver one of our country's most elite group of security professionals. There were security failures on multiple fronts." Ranking Member Jason Crow added, "It is clear that the Secret Service failed on July 13."[56]

"Over the course of twelve days—from July 2 through July 13—the Secret Service's planning and coordination for the campaign event in Butler appears to have been inadequate. According to USSS Acting Director Rowe, "the Secret Service did not give clear guidance or direction to our local law enforcement partners.[57] . . . There was no joint meeting between the Secret Service (USSS), state police, and local law enforcement (LLE) on the day of the rally."[58]

". . . [T]estimony obtained by the Task Force show that scattered meetings, vague instructions, and unclear chains of command caused confusion about the division of responsibilities—especially for local and state officers.[59] . . . the Secret Service designated the

from https://taskforce.house.gov/sites/evo-subsites/july13taskforce.house.gov/files/evo-media-document/task-force-interim-staff-report-10.21.2024.pdf, p. 10.

56. U.S. House Task Force on the Attempted Assassination of Donald J. Trump. (2024, October 21). *Interim staff report: Investigating the stunning security failures on July 13, 2024, in Butler, Pennsylvania* [PDF]. Retrieved July 16, 2025, from https://taskforce.house.gov/sites/evo-subsites/july13taskforce.house.gov/files/evo-media-document/task-force-interim-staff-report-10.21.2024.pdf, p. 10.

57. U.S. House Task Force on the Attempted Assassination of Donald J. Trump. (2024, October 21). *Interim staff report: Investigating the stunning security failures on July 13, 2024, in Butler, Pennsylvania* [PDF]. Retrieved July 16, 2025, from https://taskforce.house.gov/sites/evo-subsites/july13taskforce.house.gov/files/evo-media-document/task-force-interim-staff-report-10.21.2024.pdf, p. 10.

58. U.S. House Task Force on the Attempted Assassination of Donald J. Trump. (2024, October 21). *Interim staff report: Investigating the stunning security failures on July 13, 2024, in Butler, Pennsylvania* [PDF]. Retrieved July 16, 2025, from https://taskforce.house.gov/sites/evo-subsites/july13taskforce.house.gov/files/evo-media-document/task-force-interim-staff-report-10.21.2024.pdf, p. 10.

59. U.S. House Task Force on the Attempted Assassination of Donald J.

AGR complex, and the areas around the AGR complex, outside of the secure perimeter, despite its proximity to a main road and elevated positions from several areas on the property, including the rooftops. The USSS failed to ensure the risks associated with the AGR property were addressed, both in terms of lines of sight to the stage and as an attractive area for crowds to gather."[60]

"According to Pennsylvania State Police (PSP) Lieutenant John Herold, when the Secret Service assigned posts during a walkthrough at the Butler Farm Show property on July 11, the Secret Service did not request assets to be placed at the AGR complex, although PSP had the resources to do so. The PSP understood from the Secret Service that the Butler County Emergency Services Unit (Butler ESU) was responsible for the AGR complex. . . . Patrolman Blasko testified that he told the Secret Service his team did not have the manpower to post officers around the AGR property, and that he asked the Secret Service for additional officers to be posted there. According to Patrolman Blasko, the Secret Service said, 'they would take care of it.'"[61]

"On July 11, at 1000, the USSS led a walkthrough with PSP and local EMS, fire, and police at the Butler Farm Show. The walkthrough covered the rally stage and crowd area, and the perimeter area along the fence that divides the Butler Farm Show property from the AGR property. Witnesses who participated in the

Trump. (2024, October 21). *Interim staff report: Investigating the stunning security failures on July 13, 2024, in Butler, Pennsylvania* [PDF]. Retrieved July 16, 2025, from https://taskforce.house.gov/sites/evo-subsites/july13taskforce.house.gov/files/evo-media-document/task-force-interim-staff-report-10.21.2024.pdf, p. 11.

60. U.S. House Task Force on the Attempted Assassination of Donald J. Trump. (2024, October 21). *Interim staff report: Investigating the stunning security failures on July 13, 2024, in Butler, Pennsylvania* [PDF]. Retrieved July 16, 2025, from https://taskforce.house.gov/sites/evo-subsites/july13taskforce.house.gov/files/evo-media-document/task-force-interim-staff-report-10.21.2024.pdf, p. 11.

61. U.S. House Task Force on the Attempted Assassination of Donald J. Trump. (2024, October 21). *Interim staff report: Investigating the stunning security failures on July 13, 2024, in Butler, Pennsylvania* [PDF]. Retrieved July 16, 2025, from https://taskforce.house.gov/sites/evo-subsites/july13taskforce.house.gov/files/evo-media-document/task-force-interim-staff-report-10.21.2024.pdf, p. 11.

walkthrough told the Task Force it was disorganized. . . . the USSS did not provide any guidance as to whether or how to secure the AGR property, even after Butler Township PD Witness 1 advised PSP that his Department did not have enough manpower to station a car in the AGR parking lot during the rally."[62]

"Butler ESU led a briefing at approximately 0915 with other tactical assets from across the region. Officers from the Butler Township Police Department had a separate briefing at around 0930. The Secret Service did not participate in either briefing. . . . USSS counter snipers and LLE sniper assets spoke with each other following these briefings, but witnesses testified to the Task Force that there was no broader briefing among USSS and local or state partners, nor were they aware of an intent to hold such a briefing. In fact, a PSP trooper who was assigned to the USSS Command Post for the rally was invited to the 1000 USSS briefing by one USSS agent, then subsequently asked to leave by another.[63] . . . The lack of a unified briefing on July 13 may have led to gaps in awareness among state and local law enforcement partners as to who was stationed where, spheres of responsibility, and expectations regarding communications during the day. . . . The USSS Advance Agents did not document responsibility for securing the outer perimeter—the area outside the fence lines where individuals would be screened by magnetometers, which included the AGR building. They also did not share planning documents with state or local law enforcement, or request state or local operational plans."[64]

62. U.S. House Task Force on the Attempted Assassination of Donald J. Trump. (2024, October 21). *Interim staff report: Investigating the stunning security failures on July 13, 2024, in Butler, Pennsylvania* [PDF]. Retrieved July 16, 2025, from https://taskforce.house.gov/sites/evo-subsites/july13taskforce.house.gov/ files/evo-media-document/task-force-interim-staff-report-10.21.2024.pdf, p. 14.

63. U.S. House Task Force on the Attempted Assassination of Donald J. Trump. (2024, October 21). *Interim staff report: Investigating the stunning security failures on July 13, 2024, in Butler, Pennsylvania* [PDF]. Retrieved July 16, 2025, from https://taskforce.house.gov/sites/evo-subsites/july13taskforce.house.gov /files/evo-media-document/task-force-interim-staff-report-10.21.2024.pdf, p. 14–15.

64. U.S. House Task Force on the Attempted Assassination of Donald J.

"Local law enforcement told the Task Force that the Secret Service did not give any guidance to Butler ESU and Beaver ESU regarding the placement, role, and responsibilities of their snipers on July 13, and that in the absence of any such guidance, they understood their assignment to be overwatch of the rally venue."[65]

"Absent guidance to the contrary, and consistent with their typical role as 'marksman observers,' local ESU snipers positioned themselves inside the AGR complex, near windows facing the Butler Farm Show property, to conduct overwatch of the rally stage and crowd. The overwatch posture placed ESU personnel several feet back from the windows, looking through scopes toward the rally stage and crowd—unable to easily see the unsecured areas on the AGR property, including most of the rooftops of the AGR complex and the areas directly below the windows."[66]

"At the Task Force hearing on September 26, 2024, Ranking Member Jason Crow stated: 'The communication between the Secret Service and local and state partners was disjointed and unclear.' . . . Secret Service records show that information about a suspicious person—Crooks—at the AGR property did not reach the Secret Service command post until about 1751. By then, Crooks had been under scrutiny by the Secret Service's state and local partners for approximately 40 minutes."[67]

Trump. (2024, October 21). *Interim staff report: Investigating the stunning security failures on July 13, 2024, in Butler, Pennsylvania* [PDF]. Retrieved July 16, 2025, from https://taskforce.house.gov/sites/evo-subsites/july13taskforce.house.gov/files/evo-media-document/task-force-interim-staff-report-10.21.2024.pdf, p. 15.

65. U.S. House Task Force on the Attempted Assassination of Donald J. Trump. (2024, October 21). *Interim staff report: Investigating the stunning security failures on July 13, 2024, in Butler, Pennsylvania* [PDF]. Retrieved July 16, 2025, from https://taskforce.house.gov/sites/evo-subsites/july13taskforce.house.gov/files/evo-media-document/task-force-interim-staff-report-10.21.2024.pdf, p. 16.

66. U.S. House Task Force on the Attempted Assassination of Donald J. Trump. (2024, October 21). *Interim staff report: Investigating the stunning security failures on July 13, 2024, in Butler, Pennsylvania* [PDF]. Retrieved July 16, 2025, from https://taskforce.house.gov/sites/evo-subsites/july13taskforce.house.gov/files/evo-media-document/task-force-interim-staff-report-10.21.2024.pdf, p. 17.

67. U.S. House Task Force on the Attempted Assassination of Donald J.

"Notably, local law enforcement was not represented in the Secret Service command post. According to testimony from Butler ESU Commander Lenz, the lines of communication for July 13 were not established in advance of the event. Meanwhile, representatives from local law enforcement partner agencies—including those whose personnel first observed and engaged Crooks at the AGR property—were in a separate trailer elsewhere on the property. There was no dedicated radio link between law enforcement in the two posts, and cell connectivity issues further undermined communication during the critical period when the threat posed by Crooks rapidly escalated."

"The USSS Site Agent told the Committee that other than the local snipers inside the building, she did not know how the AGR building would be covered, but understood Butler ESU 'would have coverage of [the] building.' Butler ESU told the Committee that they informed USSS they did not have the manpower to lock down the AGR building, but USSS Advance Agents told the Committee Butler local law enforcement never raised these concerns."

"The Butler ESU officer stated that they 'did not have the manpower to lock down this area and the area [referring to the AGR building] needed to be locked down.' The Butler ESU officer told the Committee that in response to these concerns, USSS—specifically the Site Agent, Site Counterpart, and Counter Sniper Team Leader—said they 'copied' and 'they would take care of it.'"[68]

"In testimony to the Senate on July 30, 2024, Acting Director Rowe stated that a lack of communications capacity and radio

---

Trump. (2024, October 21). *Interim staff report: Investigating the stunning security failures on July 13, 2024, in Butler, Pennsylvania* [PDF]. Retrieved July 16, 2025, from https://taskforce.house.gov/sites/evo-subsites/july13taskforce.house.gov/files/evo-media-document/task-force-interim-staff-report-10.21.2024.pdf, p. 17.

68. U.S. House Task Force on the Attempted Assassination of Donald J. Trump. (2024, October 21). *Interim staff report: Investigating the stunning security failures on July 13, 2024, in Butler, Pennsylvania* [PDF]. Retrieved July 16, 2025, from https://taskforce.house.gov/sites/evo-subsites/july13taskforce.house.gov/files/evo-media-document/task-force-interim-staff-report-10.21.2024.pdf, p. 20.

interoperability challenges allowed Crooks to evade Secret Service detection. Acting Director Rowe stated that the Secret Service's internal review of the assassination attempt found an over-reliance on cell phones, instead of Secret Service radio frequencies, to communicate vital information. Local law enforcement officers, who searched for Crooks as his behavior on the AGR property became increasingly suspicious before the rally, shared information 'via mobile/cellular devices in staggered or fragmented fashion' instead of through the Secret Service's own network."[69]

"Moments before Crooks fired, a local law enforcement officer radioed that Crooks was on the roof with a gun. There is no evidence, to date, that this information reached the former President's detail, and he remained on stage."[70]

"The USSS Counter Sniper Team Leader told the Committee that if another USSS counter sniper had an issue with their post, 'they could reach out if they had any concerns. But I believe they would understand I did the advance work, this is this line of we can't see a certain threat area, I assume that the advance did his job diligently, which I did, and Hercules 1 could see the threat area.' After noticing the obstruction of the trees in front of the AGR building, one of the USSS counter snipers on Hercules 2 told the Committee that he and his partner did not notify the USSS Counter Sniper Team Leader 'because it was assumed that he took the post during his advance procedures and chose that one, regardless

69. U.S. House Task Force on the Attempted Assassination of Donald J. Trump. (2024, October 21). *Interim staff report: Investigating the stunning security failures on July 13, 2024, in Butler, Pennsylvania* [PDF]. Retrieved July 16, 2025, from https://taskforce.house.gov/sites/evo-subsites/july13taskforce.house.gov/files/evo-media-document/task-force-interim-staff-report-10.21.2024.pdf, p. 23.

70. U.S. House Task Force on the Attempted Assassination of Donald J. Trump. (2024, October 21). *Interim staff report: Investigating the stunning security failures on July 13, 2024, in Butler, Pennsylvania* [PDF]. Retrieved July 16, 2025, from https://taskforce.house.gov/sites/evo-subsites/july13taskforce.house.gov/files/evo-media-document/task-force-interim-staff-report-10.21.2024.pdf, p. 25.

of a line of sight issue with the trees, because the AGR building was to be secured by locals.'"[71]

"Butler ESU Witness 4 did send a series of text messages to Butler ESU Witness 3 at 1715 that included a description of Crooks. The final message stated: 'He has a range finder.' Butler ESU Witness 3 stated that he did not see those text messages until approximately 1740."[72]

"The fact that USSS was responsible for providing security for two protectees in the Pittsburgh area on July 13—former President Trump's event in Butler and the First Lady's event in the city of Pittsburgh—resulted in shared USSS assets at the Pittsburgh airport. Although the Site Counterpart for the Butler rally acknowledged that resources could be strained by asset sharing between protectees, she told the Committee that she was confident that there was not going to be any resource issues during this specific arrangement because she had previously worked with the local law enforcement entity providing the shared coverage."[73]

"Multiple USSS officials, including Acting Director Rowe, have acknowledged communications failures on July 13."[74]

71. U.S. House Task Force on the Attempted Assassination of Donald J. Trump. (2024, October 21). *Interim staff report: Investigating the stunning security failures on July 13, 2024, in Butler, Pennsylvania* [PDF]. Retrieved July 16, 2025, from https://taskforce.house.gov/sites/evo-subsites/july13taskforce.house.gov/files/evo-media-document/task-force-interim-staff-report-10.21.2024.pdf, p. 26.

72. U.S. House Task Force on the Attempted Assassination of Donald J. Trump. (2024, October 21). *Interim staff report: Investigating the stunning security failures on July 13, 2024, in Butler, Pennsylvania* [PDF]. Retrieved July 16, 2025, from https://taskforce.house.gov/sites/evo-subsites/july13taskforce.house.gov/files/evo-media-document/task-force-interim-staff-report-10.21.2024.pdf, p. 31.

73. U.S. House Task Force on the Attempted Assassination of Donald J. Trump. (2024, October 21). *Interim staff report: Investigating the stunning security failures on July 13, 2024, in Butler, Pennsylvania* [PDF]. Retrieved July 16, 2025, from https://taskforce.house.gov/sites/evo-subsites/july13taskforce.house.gov/files/evo-media-document/task-force-interim-staff-report-10.21.2024.pdf, p. 35.

74. U.S. House Task Force on the Attempted Assassination of Donald J. Trump. (2024, October 21). *Interim staff report: Investigating the stunning security failures on July 13, 2024, in Butler, Pennsylvania* [PDF]. Retrieved July 16, 2025,

"In an interview with the Committee, the Assistant Director of the USSS OPO said, 'Clearly, there were communication gaps that day that led to this failure. And if those communication gaps had been mitigated, information could have been passed in a more timely fashion that would've avoided that failure.'"[75]

"Butler ESU Witness 4 testified that he continued to search for Crooks from 1715 to approximately 1740. At approximately 1739, Butler ESU Witness 4 received a call from Butler ESU Witness 3 in response to the text messages from Butler ESU Witness 4. Following this call, Butler ESU Witness 4 and Beaver ESU Witness 3 decided to report their observations of Crooks to law enforcement leadership."[76]

"Prior to Butler Township PD Witness 2's transmission that Crooks was on the AGR roof, Butler Township PD Witness 5 checked with Blasko in-person and learned about the suspicious person. Butler Township PD Witness 5 was patrolling the area as part of his regular duties—he was not specifically assigned to work the rally. Butler Township PD Witness 5 then searched the water tower area and returned to Blasko."[77]

from https://taskforce.house.gov/sites/evo-subsites/july13taskforce.house.gov/files/evo-media-document/task-force-interim-staff-report-10.21.2024.pdf, p. 37.

75. U.S. House Task Force on the Attempted Assassination of Donald J. Trump. (2024, October 21). *Interim staff report: Investigating the stunning security failures on July 13, 2024, in Butler, Pennsylvania* [PDF]. Retrieved July 16, 2025, from https://taskforce.house.gov/sites/evo-subsites/july13taskforce.house.gov/files/evo-media-document/task-force-interim-staff-report-10.21.2024.pdf, p. 38.

76. U.S. House Task Force on the Attempted Assassination of Donald J. Trump. (2024, October 21). *Interim staff report: Investigating the stunning security failures on July 13, 2024, in Butler, Pennsylvania* [PDF]. Retrieved July 16, 2025, from https://taskforce.house.gov/sites/evo-subsites/july13taskforce.house.gov/files/evo-media-document/task-force-interim-staff-report-10.21.2024.pdf, p. 41.

77. U.S. House Task Force on the Attempted Assassination of Donald J. Trump. (2024, October 21). *Interim staff report: Investigating the stunning security failures on July 13, 2024, in Butler, Pennsylvania* [PDF]. Retrieved July 16, 2025, from https://taskforce.house.gov/sites/evo-subsites/july13taskforce.house.gov/files/evo-media-document/task-force-interim-staff-report-10.21.2024.pdf, p. 41.

"According to the PSP Sergeant who was stationed in the USSS Security Room, he initially told the Security Room Agent about the suspicious person with a rangefinder approximately 27 minutes prior to the shooting, and that the suspicious individual was on the AGR building roof approximately 2 minutes before the shooting. The PSP Sergeant stated that he was not aware of what, if anything, the Security Room Agent did with the information."

"Additionally, the Committee was not able to review radio communications made from the USSS Security Room because, as Acting USSS Director Rowe stated in his testimony to the Committee on July 30, the USSS did not record its radio transmissions on July 13. USSS officials told the Committee that radio communications are often recorded at protective events, but that the recording capability was not available at the rally."[78]

"Meanwhile, Butler Township Police PD Witness 4 had decided to pursue Crooks on the AGR roof and exited his patrol car. As he moved towards the AGR complex, he encountered Butler Township PD Witness 5, who helped raise Butler Township Police PD Witness 4 onto the roof."[79]

"Butler Township Police PD Witness 4 saw Crooks's weapon for the first time when Crooks turned and pointed the rifle at him. Butler Township Police PD Witness 4 testified to the Task Force that he also saw that Crooks had a bookbag and extra magazines of ammunition for a long gun. When Crooks turned to aim his rifle at Butler Township Police PD Witness 4, Butler Township Police

78. U.S. House Task Force on the Attempted Assassination of Donald J. Trump. (2024, October 21). *Interim staff report: Investigating the stunning security failures on July 13, 2024, in Butler, Pennsylvania* [PDF]. Retrieved July 16, 2025, from https://taskforce.house.gov/sites/evo-subsites/july13taskforce.house.gov/files/evo-media-document/task-force-interim-staff-report-10.21.2024.pdf, p. 41.

79. U.S. House Task Force on the Attempted Assassination of Donald J. Trump. (2024, October 21). *Interim staff report: Investigating the stunning security failures on July 13, 2024, in Butler, Pennsylvania* [PDF]. Retrieved July 16, 2025, from https://taskforce.house.gov/sites/evo-subsites/july13taskforce.house.gov/files/evo-media-document/task-force-interim-staff-report-10.21.2024.pdf, p. 42.

PD Witness 4 fell to the ground and immediately radioed that the suspicious person on the roof was armed."[80]

"USSS uses encrypted radio frequencies, which are not accessible without a USSS-issued radio. According to Butler County ESU police officers, no local law enforcement officials were given a USSS radio on July 13, and no one from USSS had a Butler County-issued radio. Similarly, all of the USSS personnel the Committee interviewed stated that they did not personally have a local radio or access to local radio channels."[81]

"To date, the Task Force has not received any evidence to suggest that message reached the former President's USSS detail prior to shots fired. The fact that Crooks was armed was reported out via the local patrol radio channel, OPS-3, which was heard by Commander Lenz, who moved to deploy Butler ESU's QRF at that time."[82]

"At 1811, Crooks fired eight rounds before being fatally shot. The evidence shows Crooks was on the roof for approximately six minutes prior to the shooting, between 1805 and 1811."[83]

80. U.S. House Task Force on the Attempted Assassination of Donald J. Trump. (2024, October 21). *Interim staff report: Investigating the stunning security failures on July 13, 2024, in Butler, Pennsylvania* [PDF]. Retrieved July 16, 2025, from https://taskforce.house.gov/sites/evo-subsites/july13taskforce.house.gov/files/evo-media-document/task-force-interim-staff-report-10.21.2024.pdf, p. 42.

81. U.S. House Task Force on the Attempted Assassination of Donald J. Trump. (2024, October 21). *Interim staff report: Investigating the stunning security failures on July 13, 2024, in Butler, Pennsylvania* [PDF]. Retrieved July 16, 2025, from https://taskforce.house.gov/sites/evo-subsites/july13taskforce.house.gov/files/evo-media-document/task-force-interim-staff-report-10.21.2024.pdf, p. 42.

82. U.S. House Task Force on the Attempted Assassination of Donald J. Trump. (2024, October 21). *Interim staff report: Investigating the stunning security failures on July 13, 2024, in Butler, Pennsylvania* [PDF]. Retrieved July 16, 2025, from https://taskforce.house.gov/sites/evo-subsites/july13taskforce.house.gov/files/evo-media-document/task-force-interim-staff-report-10.21.2024.pdf, p. 43.

83. U.S. House Task Force on the Attempted Assassination of Donald J. Trump. (2024, October 21). *Interim staff report: Investigating the stunning security failures on July 13, 2024, in Butler, Pennsylvania* [PDF]. Retrieved July 16, 2025, from https://taskforce.house.gov/sites/evo-subsites/july13taskforce.house.gov/

"USSS operated a Security Room at the July 13 rally, and Butler County law enforcement ran a separate Command Post for local law enforcement agencies. The posts were at least 120 to 300 yards distance from each other. The USSS Security Room and the local Command Post's primary means of communication with each other was by cell phone, not radio."[84]

"Butler ESU Witness 5 testified to the Task Force that he was the first law enforcement officer to return fire at Crooks. Butler ESU Witness 5 was posted on the Butler Production to Task Force, FPOTUS After Action, Beaver ESU, 22 (2024) (on file with the Task Force). Farm Show property, in the vicinity of the stage. When he heard Crooks fire an initial volley of three shots, Butler ESU Witness 5 located Crooks on the roof of the AGR complex. He fired a single shot from a standing position at Crooks, who was in a prone position on the roof. Butler ESU Witness 5 told the Task Force that he believes his shot hit Crooks. The evidence shows Crooks was struck by a single bullet (see Autopsy and Toxicology, page 48). On July 15, then-Secret Service Director Kimberly Cheatle announced that a USSS 'counter sniper team neutraliz[ed] the shooter' and there is no evidence to date to the contrary."[85]

"The USSS SAIC of the Pittsburgh Field Office did not have a working radio on his person during his entire time at the July 13 rally."[86]

---

files/evo-media-document/task-force-interim-staff-report-10.21.2024.pdf, p. 44.

84. U.S. House Task Force on the Attempted Assassination of Donald J. Trump. (2024, October 21). *Interim staff report: Investigating the stunning security failures on July 13, 2024, in Butler, Pennsylvania* [PDF]. Retrieved July 16, 2025, from https://taskforce.house.gov/sites/evo-subsites/july13taskforce.house.gov/files/evo-media-document/task-force-interim-staff-report-10.21.2024.pdf, p. 44.

85. U.S. House Task Force on the Attempted Assassination of Donald J. Trump. (2024, October 21). *Interim staff report: Investigating the stunning security failures on July 13, 2024, in Butler, Pennsylvania* [PDF]. Retrieved July 16, 2025, from https://taskforce.house.gov/sites/evo-subsites/july13taskforce.house.gov/files/evo-media-document/task-force-interim-staff-report-10.21.2024.pdf, pp. 44–45.

86. U.S. House Task Force on the Attempted Assassination of Donald J.

"Having given the Lead Advance Agent his working radio and unable to code the Lead Advance Agent's radio, the SAIC did not have direct access to any radio communications with other USSS agents while he was at the rally."[87]

"Acting Director Rowe testified before the joint HSGAC and Judiciary Committee hearing on July 30, 2024, that the outage of the C-UAS system had cost him 'a lot of sleep because of the eventual outcome of the assailant.' Acting Director Rowe testified that perhaps had the CUAS system been operational at 3:51 pm, USSS agents would have spoken with Crooks and he could have decided not to go through with his assassination attempt."[88]

"The FBI identified the weapon used by Crooks as an AR style rifle, and announced that his phone as well as explosive devices found in his car had been shipped to Quantico for forensic analysis. The FBI also reported that Crooks' social media history going back to 2019 espoused political violence. Crooks also prepared for July 13, searching online for details on how to build an explosive and researching how the rally would be set up."[89]

Trump. (2024, October 21). *Interim staff report: Investigating the stunning security failures on July 13, 2024, in Butler, Pennsylvania* [PDF]. Retrieved July 16, 2025, from https://taskforce.house.gov/sites/evo-subsites/july13taskforce.house.gov/files/evo-media-document/task-force-interim-staff-report-10.21.2024.pdf, p. 48.

87. U.S. House Task Force on the Attempted Assassination of Donald J. Trump. (2024, October 21). *Interim staff report: Investigating the stunning security failures on July 13, 2024, in Butler, Pennsylvania* [PDF]. Retrieved July 16, 2025, from https://taskforce.house.gov/sites/evo-subsites/july13taskforce.house.gov/files/evo-media-document/task-force-interim-staff-report-10.21.2024.pdf, p. 49.

88. U.S. House Task Force on the Attempted Assassination of Donald J. Trump. (2024, October 21). *Interim staff report: Investigating the stunning security failures on July 13, 2024, in Butler, Pennsylvania* [PDF]. Retrieved July 16, 2025, from https://taskforce.house.gov/sites/evo-subsites/july13taskforce.house.gov/files/evo-media-document/task-force-interim-staff-report-10.21.2024.pdf, p. 71.

89. U.S. House Task Force on the Attempted Assassination of Donald J. Trump. (2024, October 21). *Interim staff report: Investigating the stunning security failures on July 13, 2024, in Butler, Pennsylvania* [PDF]. Retrieved July 16, 2025, from https://taskforce.house.gov/sites/evo-subsites/july13taskforce.house.gov/files/evo-media-document/task-force-interim-staff-report-10.21.2024.pdf, p. 73.

"Prior to the Butler rally, Crooks had researched multiple political targets including President Biden, former President Trump, the DNC Convention, and the RNC Convention. On July 6, the same day Crooks registered for the Butler rally, he searched online with the following entry: 'how far away was Oswald from Kennedy.'"[90]

"AGR Sniper 1 (Beaver County) posted in a window inside the AGR building observed an individual outside walk by the window, who the sniper later determined was Crooks. This was the first confirmed sighting of Crooks by law enforcement, 1 hour and 1 minute before the shooting."[91]

[at 5:44pm] "The Butler ESU Commander called a PSP Sergeant, stationed in the USSS Security Room, who was his primary point-of-contact and liaison to USSS. In a subsequent interview, the PSP Sergeant stated he received information about a suspicious person near the AGR building, specifically, 'a young white male, long hair, with a rangefinder, like, had been seen by the counter snipers. . . . And then he also said a bike and a backpack had appeared that they weren't sure was related, but wasn't there, obviously, at the start of the rally.' This was the first confirmed communication to USSS about Crooks, approximately 27 minutes before the shooting."[92]

90. U.S. House Task Force on the Attempted Assassination of Donald J. Trump. (2024, October 21). *Interim staff report: Investigating the stunning security failures on July 13, 2024, in Butler, Pennsylvania* [PDF]. Retrieved July 16, 2025, from https://taskforce.house.gov/sites/evo-subsites/july13taskforce.house.gov/files/evo-media-document/task-force-interim-staff-report-10.21.2024.pdf, p. 74.

91. U.S. House Task Force on the Attempted Assassination of Donald J. Trump. (2024, October 21). *Interim staff report: Investigating the stunning security failures on July 13, 2024, in Butler, Pennsylvania* [PDF]. Retrieved July 16, 2025, from https://taskforce.house.gov/sites/evo-subsites/july13taskforce.house.gov/files/evo-media-document/task-force-interim-staff-report-10.21.2024.pdf, p. 75.

92. U.S. House Task Force on the Attempted Assassination of Donald J. Trump. (2024, October 21). *Interim staff report: Investigating the stunning security failures on July 13, 2024, in Butler, Pennsylvania* [PDF]. Retrieved July 16, 2025, from https://taskforce.house.gov/sites/evo-subsites/july13taskforce.house.gov/files/evo-media-document/task-force-interim-staff-report-10.21.2024.pdf, p. 77.

"DHS and the USSS continue to provide heavily redacted or incomplete documents and productions in response to the Committee's bipartisan inquiry. On July 24 and 25, 2024, the Committee requested information on planning, resources, intelligence, and related communications for each, as well as transcribed interviews with 13 USSS individuals and teams connected to the Butler rally."[93]

"A Senate inquiry found that responsibility and authority for planning and security decisions for the July 13 campaign rally was not clearly assigned or documented; an independent panel reviewing the failures that led to the attempted assassination called on the Secret Service to replace its leadership with people from the private sector and focus almost exclusively on its protective mission; and the Secret Service's own internal investigation found that complacency had set in among some of the agents charged with securing the rally site"[94]

In sum, a "The Media never lie" post sums the tragic, epic failure. Never in history has such an amateur gone so far, so blatantly, and so close to murdering a former President.

The initial blame game against the local police, shifting responsibility solely upon local enforcement with the task of securing properties surrounding the speaking site, culminated in an excoriating condemnation of wanton negligence by the Secret Service on many levels,[95] and the forced resignation of the Director.

93. U.S. House Task Force on the Attempted Assassination of Donald J. Trump. (2024, October 21). *Interim staff report: Investigating the stunning security failures on July 13, 2024, in Butler, Pennsylvania* [PDF]. Retrieved July 16, 2025, from https://taskforce.house.gov/sites/evo-subsites/july13taskforce.house.gov/files/evo-media-document/task-force-interim-staff-report-10.21.2024.pdf, p. 86.

94. The New York Times. (2024, October 21). *Secret Service report outlines breakdowns in communications and oversight before Trump rally shooting. The New York Times.* https://www.nytimes.com/2024/10/21/us/politics/secret-service-trump-butler-house-report.html?searchResultPosition=2.

95. Victoria Churchill & Alex Oliveira, *Secret Service blames local police, says they were tasked with securing properties surrounding Trump's Pa. rally*, N.Y. Post, July 14, 2024, https://nypost.com/2024/07/14/us-news/secret-service-blames

As of December 2024 Fox News reported a further, heated, loud, and boisterous shouting match on the floor of Congress during interrogation of the U.S. Secret Service:

> "Who is usually at an event like this closest to the President of the United States?" Fallon asked, pointing at the photo. "Were you the special agent in charge of the detail that day?"
>
> Rowe said the security detail was present but out of view of the camera. As he spoke, he became enraged and accused Fallon of using 9/11 for political purposes.
>
> "That is the day where we remember more than 3,000 people that have died on 9/11. I actually responded to Ground Zero," Rowe said. "I was there going through the ashes of the World Trade Center."
>
> "I'm not asking that, I'm asking you, if you were . . . were you the special agent in charge!?" Fallon interrupted, shouting at Rowe.
>
> Rowe raised his voice in response. "I was there to show respect for a Secret Service member that died on 9/11!" he yelled back.
>
> "Do not invoke 9/11 for political purposes!" Rowe screamed at the lawmaker.
>
> "I'm not," Fallon fired back, as the committee chairman demanded order and banged his gavel.
>
> "You are, sir. You are out of line, congressman!" Rowe fumed. "Way out of line."
>
> Fallon then accused Rowe of "playing politics" by refusing to answer his question.
>
> "I am a public servant who has served this nation," Rowe retorted, saying he served on the nation's "darkest day."
>
> "You will not politicize it!" Rowe thundered.[96]

-local-police-says-it-was-tasked-with-securing-properties-surrounding-trumps-pa-rally/.

96. Fox News Channel. (2024, December 5). *WATCH EXCHANGE: Secret Service Director Ronald Rowe spars with GOP Rep. Pat Fallon* [Video segment]. *The Faulkner Focus.* https://www.foxnews.com/video/6365587186112.

Many questions remain as to who should have done what, should have done when, and should have done how, obfuscated, of course, by proverbial blame games, dodged elusive non-answers, passing the buck, sandbagging, stonewalling, and simple silence. Bureaucracies have a way of covering for themselves—one of their ways and means of self-preservation.

Conclusion

The public verdict is in—gross negligence, wanton negligence, extreme negligence, inexcusable negligence, surprising negligence, so much so, some supposed that the failures were intentional, to allow a political undesirable to be open to a possible elimination. No evidence is dispositive, however, that that any law enforcement of any entity intentionally allowed the tragedy. But of course, some things cannot be proved.

THEOLOGICAL ANALYSIS

The whole of Scripture includes numerous tragedies, including tragedies of political assassinations. Although "thou shalt love thy neighbor as thyself" is a core, central social ethic and categorical imperative of both Testaments (Lev. 19:18b[1]), the ethical summary of the Torah as per both the Lord Jesus Christ (Matt. 19:19; 22:39; Mark 12:31; Luke 10:27), Apostle Paul (Rom. 13:9b; Gal. 5:14), and Apostle James (James 2:8), hate-motivated murder tragically traumatized the second generation since Creation—Abel's blood would "cry from the ground" (Gen. 4:10; Heb. 11:4; 12:24). "No one can feel hatred towards those for whom he prays" preached the Church Father John Chrysostom, but both the Hebrew Bible and Greek New Testament are realistic in their apprehension of true human nature (*cf.* Gen. 6:5).

Despite David's abhorrence of assassination (2 Sam. 4:9–12) and Mosaic law prohibiting assassination (Deut. 27:24), instances of assassination are replete in the Hebrew Bible: (1) Eglon, by Ehud, in Judges 3:15–22; (2) Abner, by Joab, in 2 Sam. 3:27; (3) Ish-bosheth, by the sons of Rimmon, in 2 Sam. 4:5–7; (4) Amnon, by Absalom, in 2 Sam. 13:28–29; (5) Amasa, by Joab, 2 Sam. 20:9–10; (6) Joash, by his servants, in 2 Kings 12:20; (7) Sennacherib, by his sons, in 2 Kings 19:37 and Isaiah 37:38, as well as Gedaliah by Ishmael son of Nethaniah, and the ten assassins who were his accomplices, together with most of the Jews who had joined him

---

1. Leviticus 19:18b: "וְאָהַבְתָּ לְרֵעֲךָ כָּמוֹךָ אֲנִי יְהוָה" *The Lexham Hebrew Bible* (Bellingham, WA: Lexham Press, 2012), Lev. 19:18.

and many Babylonians whom Nebuchadnezzar left in service with Gedaliah in Jeremiah 41:2–3.[2]

The Assassination of Eglon, King of Moab—circa 1300–1275 B.C.

Although the first recorded murder in human history, the Genesis 4 murder of Abel by his older brother Cain (*cf.* Gen. 4:10; Heb. 11:4; 12:24), is arguably an intrafamilial assassination, because of the absence in that point in the history of the Hebrew Bible of a political structure, the first recorded political assassination in the Hebrew Bible, Eglon, King of Moab[3] by the Benjamite judge-deliverer Ehud ben-Gera (son of Gera), referenced in Judges 3:12–20, will be the first analysis of political assassinations in the Hebrew Bible.

The name of Eglon, King of Moab (עֶגְלוֹן, *eglon*), *circa* 1300–1275 B.C., bears a protruding significance[4]—his name is related

2. James Swanson and Orville Nave, *New Nave's Topical Bible* (Oak Harbor: Logos Research Systems, 1994).

3. "Rabbinic tradition identifies Eglon as both the grandson of Balak, the Moabite king who hired Balaam to curse Israel (Numbers 22–24), and the father or grandfather of Ruth (*Ruth Targum* 1:4; for further references see Levine 1973: 48 n. 6). Aggadic commentary finds a redeeming virtue in Eglon's effort to stand at the 'word of God' (Judg 3:20). According to this tradition, the king's pious action received its reward through the inclusion of Ruth in the genealogy of David (Ruth 4:18–22; see *Ruth Rabbah* 2.9; note 1 Sam 22:3–4). Furthermore, because of Ruth's own piety, she would be the ancestor of 'the six Righteous of the world,' namely, 'David, Daniel, his three companions, and the Messiah king' (*Ruth Targum* 3:15). Perhaps the familiarity of the latter tradition also contributed to the inclusion of Ruth in the otherwise selective genealogy of Jesus (Matt 1:5; cf. Luke 3:32)." John Kutsko, Ph.D. Student, Harvard University, Cambridge, MA, "Eglon (Person)," *The Anchor Yale Bible Dictionary* (New York: Doubleday, 1992) 319–320.

4. "Eglon" was also the name of a Canaanite city whose king entered an alliance with four other Canaanite rulers against the Gibeonites (Josh. 10:3), who had made, although via subterfuge and fraud, a treaty with Israel (Joshua 9). The city of Eglon was captured by the Israelite army under Joshua and became a part of the territory of the tribe of Judah. Many, if not most, scholars have held that the modern site of Tell el-Hesi was the location of ancient Eglon (although some have

to the Hebrew word for calf (עֵגֶל, *egel*) and heifer (עֶגְלָה, *eglah*). The alliteration and implied wordplay may imply Eglon as a fatted calf (עֵגֶל) prepared for slaughter and consumption, as well as dull, dim-witted ox (עֶגְלָה).[5] "The native reader (or hearer) would immediately catch the play on Eglon's name, which recalls both 'calf' (*'ēgel, 'eglâ*) and 'rotund' (*'āgôl, 'āgōl*). The description of Eglon as 'very fat' (*bārî' mĕ'ōd*, v 17), is echoed in the description of his troops as 'plump' or 'fat' (*šāmēn*, v 29). (Note also the lines in the Ugaritic Kirta story [*KTU* 1.15 IV:4, 15]: *šmn mri*, 'fattest of the fatlings,' in which *šāmēn* modifies *mĕrî'*, a form V 2, p 320 phonetically related to *bārî'*, 'fat.')."[6]

Implied mockery of morbid obesity is woven in the Hebrew narrative—the imagery of a ineffectual, immobile, ineffective, and perhaps effeminate caricature (so Niditch, Butler, Block)[7] implies weakness, in contradistinction to Ehud's focus, fortitude, and finesse. Commentators Stone in "Eglon's Belly" and Neef in "Eglon als 'Kälbermann'?" both disagree, that "lampooning"[8] Ehud's target would diminish Ehud's image of purpose, prowess, and power. Judges 3:17 describes Eglon as extremely obese (בָּרִיא, *bari'*), translated by most English translations as "fat." Although both Septuagint recensions translate בָּרִיא as ἀστεῖος (*asteîos*), meaning "handsome," Niditch and Butler interpret the term as a comical[9] *double entendre*, that Eglon was at least "well fed" if not overfed,

contended for Tell ʿEton). Both proposed locations are southwest of Lachish. See *Ehud; Joshua; Judges.* See *Holman Illustrated Bible Dictionary*, s.v. "Eglon."

5. Kerry Lee, "Eglon, King of Moab," *The Lexham Bible Dictionary* (Bellingham, WA: Lexham Press, 2016).

6. John Kutsko, Ph.D. Student, Harvard University, Cambridge, MA, "Eglon (Person)," *The Anchor Yale Bible Dictionary* (New York: Doubleday, 1992), 319–320.

7. Kerry Lee, "Eglon, King of Moab," *The Lexham Bible Dictionary* (Bellingham, WA: Lexham Press, 2016).

8. Kerry Lee, "Eglon, King of Moab," *The Lexham Bible Dictionary* (Bellingham, WA: Lexham Press, 2016).

9. Cf. L. K. Handy, "Uneasy Laughter: Ehud and Eglon as Ethnic Humor." *SJOT* 6 (1992), 233–246

even to the point of gluttony.[10] He appears in modern parlance in the genre of Jabba the Hut. Implied extreme self-indulgence exudes in Judges 3:22, where the gripped handle of Ehud's knife penetrates Eglon's gut to the point the entire weapon is buried in Eglon's fat (חֵלֶב, *chelev*) which closes up over and upon the whole weapon. Ehud is apparently left-handed like many Benjamites (cf. Judges 20:16).[11]

Ehud is the second judge-deliverer ("savior" *môšîʿa;* Judg 3:12–30) in the book of Judges, who spearheads a command-and-control decapitation of a leader, Eglon, who was able to forge a coalition of Moabites, Ammonites, and Amalekites, which established the historic and strategic Jericho, the "City of Palms," as a base of operations. At the power base, apparently, tribute from the subjugated was received.[12] In the ninth century, as per the Mesha Stele, Moab, when subjugated, paid tribute.[13] Regarding Jericho, "(1) when the Israelites conquered the city the walls collapsed (Josh. 6:20), (2) the Israelites burned the city (Josh. 6:24), and (3) the city was probably reoccupied shortly after the Conquest, first by the Benjamites, and then by Eglon (*ca.* 1320 B.C. according to the chronology of Judges; Josh. 18:21; Judges 3:12–14)."[14]

10. Niditch, *Judges*, 43–54; Butler, *Judges*, 54; see also Webb, *The Book of Judges*, 129–130, as quoted in Kerry Lee, "Eglon, King of Moab," *The Lexham Bible Dictionary* (Bellingham, WA: Lexham Press, 2016). Susannaan Niditch, *Judges: A Commentary*. The Old Testament Library. Westminster John Knox Press, 2008. Trent Butler, *Judges. Word Biblical Commentary* 8. Nashville: Thomas Nelson Publishers, 2009. Barry G. Webb, *The Book of Judges: An Integrated Reading*. Journal for the Study of the Old Testament Supplement Series 46. Sheffield, England: *Journal for the Study of the Old Testament Press*, 1987.

11. E. D. Isaacs, "Eglon," *The International Standard Bible Encyclopedia, Revised* (Wm. B. Eerdmans, 1979–1988), 28.

12. See Soggin, *Judges* OTL, 52–54; Knauf 1988: 64; Josephus, *Antiquities* 5.187; compare Soggin, J. A. 1989. ʾEhud und ʿEglon: Bemerkungen zu Richter III 11b–31. *VT* 39: 95–100.

13. In the 9th century B.C., the situation was reversed when Mesha, king of Moab, was obliged to deliver tribute to the king of Israel until he successfully overthrew Israelite domination (2 Kings 3; note also Mesha Stelde [*KAI* #181; *ANET*, pp. 320–21, esp. lines 1–9]).

14. Bruce K. Waltke, "Palestinian Artifactual Evidence Supporting the Early Date of the Exodus," *Bibliotheca Sacra* 129 (1972), 39.

Eglon's successful alliance between Moabites, Ammonites, and Amalekites dominated and oppressed Israel with tribute for eighteen (18) years. The suffering people of Israel "at length" "cried unto the Lord" in their distress, and he "raised them up a deliverer" (מוֹשִׁיעַ) in the commander of Israelite forces, Ehud, the son of Gera, a Benjamite.[15]

Subtly, Ehud ben-Gera (son of Gera), literally "son of the right" (Benjamite) adds irony to the lefthanded[16] terminator of the self-indulgent overlord. Ehud puts the proverbial carrot before the horse by dangling the cryptic "secret message from God" (or "thing," děbar-sēter) before the previously unchallenged overlord. Bringing Israelite tribute to Eglon, he claims to bear a secret message for the king.

The course of the series of events revolving around the cryptic private message from God is enriched by ironic wordplay. Ehud's front—his pretext for a private audience with the king—is a strikingly ironic extended pun on his covert intention: Ehud's "word" (dābār, vv 19, 20) which he has for Eglon is, in a sense, "spoken" by the dagger's two edges (pēyôt, lit. "mouths," v 16).[17] Similarly, the narrative balances the dramatic action around a single verb: Ehud's "thrusting" (tqʿ) the sword into Eglon's belly (v 21) is followed by his "blowing" (tqʿ) the trumpet to rally the Israelites and complete the coup d'état (v 27).[18]

After Ehud stabs Eglon, leaving the dagger lodged in his belly, v 22b adds the phrase wayyēṣēʾ happaršědōnâ. However, paršědōnâ is a hapax legomenon which has been variously interpreted. The

15. M. G. Easton, *Illustrated Bible Dictionary and Treasury of Biblical History, Biography, Geography, Doctrine, and Literature* (New York: Harper & Brothers, 1893), 212.

16. John Kutsko, Ph.D. Student, Harvard University, Cambridge, MA, "Eglon (Person)," *The Anchor Yale Bible Dictionary* (New York: Doubleday, 1992), 319–320.

17. John Kutsko, Ph.D. Student, Harvard University, Cambridge, MA, "Eglon (Person)," *The Anchor Yale Bible Dictionary* (New York: Doubleday, 1992), 319–320.

18. For further observations on these and other features of the narrative art of this episode, see Alonso-Schökel (1961),148–58 and Alter (1981), 37–41.

RSV translates this as "dirt" (i.e., feces), in the phrase, "and the dirt came out," the result of either the puncturing of the colon, or a post-mortem release of the intestines.[19] Halpern translates it as "anal sphinchter."[20] The LXX omits the phrase entirely. Whatever the exact meaning of *paršĕdōnâ* in the Eglon-Ehud story, the context seems to indicate some sort of "bowel movement" as a result of the death blow, since his guards later assume that he is relieving himself when they find the door locked (vv 24–25).[21] "The scatological details of the assassination, highlighting the humiliating effectiveness of the deed (vv 21–23), heighten the satire of the story. Even the description of the confused guards in vv 24–25 borders on slapstick, were it not for the sobering discovery on the other side of the door."[22]

Eglon received tribute from Ehud at his base of operations, where apparently he basked in a sense of security.[23] "By deceit and clever punning, the Benjaminite manipulates Eglon into a situation where he may be murdered without recourse to his guards."[24]

19. *Jonathan* and Vulgate; see Moore George Foot. *A Critical and Exegetical Commentary on Judges.* International Critical Commentary. Edinburgh: T & T Clark, 1910), 97.

20. Baruch Halpern, *The First Historians: The Hebrew Bible and History,* Ancient Israel and Its Literature (University Park, PA: Penn State University Press, 1996), 40, 69 n. 3.

21. John Kutsko, Ph.D. Student, Harvard University, Cambridge, MA, "Eglon (Person)," *The Anchor Yale Bible Dictionary* (New York: Doubleday, 1992) 319–320: "Perhaps the episode of Joab's execution of Amasa in 2 Samuel 20 may shed light on this incident. The actions and outcome are remarkably similar to the Eglon-Ehud story: Joab approaches Amasa, grasps Amasa's beard with his right hand to kiss him, and with his left hand he reaches for the dagger hidden under his garment (vv. 8–10a). Only one thrust of the blade is needed (v 10b), and Amasa "shed his bowels *(mē'āyw)* to the ground.""

22. John Kutsko, Ph.D. Student, Harvard University, Cambridge, MA, "Eglon (Person)," *The Anchor Yale Bible Dictionary* (New York: Doubleday, 1992), 319–320.

23. Josephus *Ant* 5.187; see Soggin *Judges* OTL, 53–54); John Kutsko, "Eglon (Person)," *The Anchor Yale Bible Dictionary* (New York: Doubleday, 1992), 319–320.

24. E. A. Knauf, "Eglon and Orpah," *JSOT* 51 (1991): 25–44; Daniel C. Browning Jr., "Eglon," *Eerdmans Dictionary of the Bible* (Grand Rapids, Mich.:

This assassination protrudes as piercing locked-in murder, where the overlord perhaps stood to receive annual tribute, perhaps from the vassal in obeisance, only receive a grueling, fatal abdominal wound.[25] Eglon sends out everyone from his presence except Ehud, as if he feels overly secure, without any sense of threat. In an ironic twist, Ehud then assassinates Eglon by thrusting a knife so far into his belly that the handle goes in after the blade and Eglon's fat closes in over it.[26] The guards delay and tarry, pondering whether their overlord is relieving himself.

The power play between Ehud and his target Eglon is a duel, a fight to the finish, clashing and colliding opposing forces—mission focus versus self-indulgent fatness, situational awareness versus situational unawareness, precise strategy versus flawed defense, professional competence versus unprofessional slackness, and resilient constancy versus lackadaisical slackness.

The Assassination of Abner, Commander of Israelite Forces Under Both Saul and His Son Ishbosheth (a/k/a Eshbaal)—circa. 1000 B.C.

The tragic demise of Abner (אַבְנֵר, *avner*, אֲבִינֵר, *aviner*) is one of the low points in the subterrain of the Hebrew Bible. Abner, commander of armed forces under the failed and failing Saulite dynasty, pledged his new loyalty to the first of the Davidic royal line, to King David himself: "And Abner sent messengers to David on his behalf, saying, Whose *is* the land? saying *also*, Make thy league with me, and, behold, my hand *shall be* with thee, to bring about all Israel unto thee" (2 Sam. 3:12).[27] Literally, "Abner" means father

W.B. Eerdmans, 2000), 375.

25. See B. Halpern, "The Assassination of Eglon: The First Locked-Room Murder Mystery," in *BRev* 4/6 [Dec. 1988], 32–41, 44.

26. Kerry Lee, "Eglon, King of Moab," *The Lexham Bible Dictionary* (Bellingham, WA: Lexham Press, 2016).

27. *The Holy Bible: King James Version*, Electronic Edition of the 1900 Authorized Version. (Bellingham, WA: Logos Research Systems, Inc., 2009), 2 Sam. 3–4:1.

of light; i.e., "enlightening," the son of Ner and uncle of Saul, who served as commander of Saul's army, only second to the King himself (1 Sam. 14:50; 17:55; 20:25).[28] The name means "father is Ner" or "father is a lamp." The variant form "Abiner" means "my father is Ner"; "my father is a lamp."[29] He first introduced David to the court of Saul after the victory over Goliath (1 Sam. 17:57).[30] Previously, as per his original loyalty/fealty, Abner, the son of Ner, led the son of Saul, Ish-bosheth (a/k/a Eshbaal), "over to Mahanaim" and coronated him King in Gilead, ruling "over the Ashurites," "over Jezreel, and over Ephraim, and over Benjaman, and over all Israel" (2 Sam. 2:8–10).[31] Abner is one of the few officials listed as part of Saul's court.[32] Despite such prestige, position, power, and prominence, David would eventually lament over such a tragic, ignominious demise: "Died Abner as a fool dieth?" (2 Sam. 3:32a).[33] From regal height to dusty depth, David further lamented, "Thy hands were not bound, Nor thy feet put into fetter: As a man falleth before wicked men, so fellest thou" (2 Sam. 3:34).[34]

28. M. G. Easton, *Illustrated Bible Dictionary and Treasury of Biblical History, Biography, Geography, Doctrine, and Literature* (New York: Harper & Brothers, 1893), 9.

29. Diana V. Edelman, "Abner (Person)," *The Anchor Yale Bible Dictionary* (New York: Doubleday, 1992), 26–28.

30. M. G. Easton, *Illustrated Bible Dictionary and Treasury of Biblical History, Biography, Geography, Doctrine, and Literature* (New York: Harper & Brothers, 1893), 9.

31. *The Holy Bible: King James Version*, Electronic Edition of the 1900 Authorized Version. (Bellingham, WA: Logos Research Systems, Inc., 2009), 2 Sam. 3–4:1.

32. R. P. Gordon, M.A., Ph.D., Lecturer in Old Testament, University of Cambridge, "Abner," *New Bible Dictionary* (Leicester, England; Downers Grove, IL: InterVarsity Press, 1996), 4.

33. *The Holy Bible: King James Version*, Electronic Edition of the 1900 Authorized Version. (Bellingham, WA: Logos Research Systems, Inc., 2009), 2 Sam. 3–4:1.

34. *The Holy Bible: King James Version*, Electronic Edition of the 1900 Authorized Version. (Bellingham, WA: Logos Research Systems, Inc., 2009), 2 Sam. 3–4:1.

The kernel of the tragedy of Abner is a cycle: (1) Beginning: Abner was born into royalty in the tribe of Benjaman, as his nephew Saul (1 Sam. 14:50) was anointed by the prophet Samuel (*cf.* 1 Samuel 10). (2) Succession: After the military defeat and consequent deaths of Saul and his favored son Jonathan, as well as his sons Abinadab and Malchi-shua (*cf.* 1 Samuel 31) on Mount Gilboa at the hands of the mortal enemies, the Philistines (Amos 9:7; Jer. 47:4), Abner maintained his loyalty to the hereditary ruling Benjamite caste, and committed wholeheartedly to Saul's successor, Ish-bosheth (a/k/a Eshbaal or Ishbaal) (2 Sam. 2:8). Civil war ensued between the Saulite and Davidic lines, while David's nephews Joab and Asahel led the charge against Abner and Ish-bosheth. During the pursuit, Abner killed Asahel in apparent self-defense (2 Sam. 2:12–32).[35] (3) Transfer: However, Ish-bosheth rushed to judgment, accusing Abner of treason for taking one of his father Saul's concubines (2 Sam. 3:7–8),[36] which moved Abner to righteous indignation. As the leadership of Ish-bosheth was flailing, floundering, and failing, Abner appeared to have designs to take leadership via the symbolic act of taking, publicly (as Absolam had done against David), one of Saul's concubines, Rizpah, as "access to the royal harem indicated one's rightful claim to the throne"[37] (*cf.* 2 Sam. 16:20–23). Ironically, Ish-bosheth's father Saul was prone to crass rashness and false accusation—Saul falsely accused David of treason rashly (*cf.* Prov. 18:13: "He that answereth a matter before he heareth it, it is folly and shame unto him"). (4) Inauguration: Consequently, Abner "transferred"—he applied to, and was accepted by, David for the job of commander of all Israelite armed forces—which, in turn, infuriated David's nephew, Joab, previous commander of all of David's armed forces. (5) Termination: Joab then deceived and destroyed his replacement in the gate of Hebron (2 Sam. 3:27), not unlike Cain's murderous treachery against his

---

35. Jeremiah K. Garrett, "Abner, Son of Ner," *The Lexham Bible Dictionary* (Bellingham, WA: Lexham Press, 2016).

36. *Holman Illustrated Bible Dictionary*, s.v. "Abner."

37. Paul S. Ash, "Abner," *Eerdmans Dictionary of the Bible* (Grand Rapids, Mich.: W.B. Eerdmans, 2000), 8.

brother Abel (*cf.* Genesis 4). Partially, Joab avenges his brother's death; fully, he eliminates his competition (2 Sam. 2:18–23).

When Saul and his three sons fell in battle on Mount Gilboa, Abner took the initiative to restore central leadership. He took up the cause of the young heir to the throne, Ishbosheth, whom he forthwith removed from the neighborhood of David to Mahanaim in the east Jordan country. There Abner proclaimed him king over all Israel. By the pool of Gibeon he and his men met Joab and the servants of David. Twelve men on each side engaged in combat, which ended disastrously for Abner, who fled. He was pursued by Asahel, Joab's brother, whom Abner killed in self-defense—after warning. "Though Joab and his brother Abishai sought to avenge their brother's death on the spot, a truce was effected; Abner was permitted to go his way after 360 of his men had fallen . . . . Joab naturally awaited his opportunity."[38] Joab had his revenge "for the blood of Asahel his brother (literally 'made by God' or 'God has made')" (2 Sam. 3:27). Truly, politics is "dirty business."

David's soul-stirring lament of the pathos of Abner's assassination echoes—"Know ye not that there is a prince and a great man fallen this day in Israel?" (2 Sam. 3:33–38.)[39] The good may fall by evil, and their good turns to a sad memory. Joab's murder of his replacement nevertheless served to consolidate David's hold on power, as "the backbone of the opposition to David was broken."[40] The pragmatism of politics tends to minimize the assize of dreadful evils.

38. M. L. Margolis, "Abner," *The International Standard Bible Encyclopedia, Revised* (Wm. B. Eerdmans, 1979–1988), 12–13.

39. M. G. Easton, *Illustrated Bible Dictionary and Treasury of Biblical History, Biography, Geography, Doctrine, and Literature* (New York: Harper & Brothers, 1893), 9.

40. Max L. Margolis, "Abner," *The International Standard Bible Encyclopaedia* (Chicago: The Howard-Severance Company, 1915), 14–15.

The Assassination of the Son of Saul, Ish-bosheth, a/k/a Esh-baal—1004 B.C.

Esh-baal literally means "man of Baal," or "Baal exists" (1 Chron. 8:33; 9:39). [41] During the period of the judges and the early monarchy many Hebrew names were compounded with "baal," a word that can mean "master" or "possessor." [42] Later generations were reluctant to speak the name "baal," so "bosheth" (shame) was substituted (cf. Hosea 2:16–17). Thus Esh-baal was altered to Ish-bosheth (2 Sam. 2:8), which means "man of shame."[43]

The name (2 Samuel 2–4) is commonly thought to have been Eshbaal originally, altered by scribes who wrote bošet ('shame') instead of the apparently pagan divine name Baal. In 1 Chron. 8:33, 9:39 the form Eshbaal is written. Recently a strong case has been argued against this view, bošet being understood as a divine attribute, 'pride, strength'. Ishbosheth and Eshbaal would be alternative names for one man (so, too, Mephibosheth and Meribbaal; see M. Tsevat, HUCA 46, 1975, pp. 71–87). A son of Saul, the Ishvi of 1 Sam. 14:49 (a corruption of Isaiah, i.e. Ishbaal), he was made king of Israel at Mahanaim, out of reach of the Philistines, by Abner, his father's commander.[44]

The different names in 2 Samuel and 1 Chronicles have led to scholarly discussions about monotheism in early Israel and the biblical authors' views of Saul. [45] It is possible that Saul worshiped the Canaanite deity Baal along with Yahweh and therefore named

41. Walter A. Elwell and Barry J. Beitzel, "Esh-Baal," *Baker Encyclopedia of the Bible* (Grand Rapids, Mich.: Baker Book House, 1988), 717–718.

42. *Baker Encyclopedia of the Bible*, ed. Walter A. Elwell (Grand Rapids: Baker, 1988), 717–718.

43. Walter A. Elwell and Barry J. Beitzel, "Esh-Baal," *Baker Encyclopedia of the Bible* (Grand Rapids, Mich.: Baker Book House, 1988), 717–718.

44. A. R. Millard, M.A., M.Phil., F.S.A., Rankin Reader in Hebrew and Ancient Semitic Languages, University of Liverpool, "Ishbosheth," *New Bible Dictionary* (Leicester, England; Downers Grove, IL: InterVarsity Press, 1996), 518–519.ss, 1996), 518–519.

45. Chris Stevens, "Ish-Bosheth, Son of Saul," *The Lexham Bible Dictionary* (Bellingham, WA: Lexham Press, 2016).

his son "Eshbaal" ("man of Baal" or "Baal exists"). However, scholars often note that *baal* could be used generically to mean "lord" and does not necessarily imply polytheism (Anderson, *2 Samuel*, 32). Avioz suggests that even if Saul was referring to the Canaanite god, he might not have viewed this as a contradiction to monotheism (Avioz, "Names," 19–20). [46] Hinson suggests that the author of Samuel substituted "Ish-Bosheth" ("man of shame") because, after years of interaction with Canaanite religion, he did not want to use a name associated with Baal. (Hinson, *History*, 91–92). In this view, when Chronicles was written later, the original name "Eshbaal" was recovered in an attempt to cast Saul in a negative light: Naming his son after a foreign deity makes him appear idolatrous. Thus, both names may be seen as examples of dysphemism—the intentional alteration of a term for disparaging purposes. [47] Alternatively, Hamilton (among others) suggests that there is no such substitution since *boshet* is equivalent to *baal* (Hamilton, "New Evidence"). This view depends heavily on loan words from Akkadian, Amorite, and other Semitic languages, however, and has not been widely accepted. [48]

The Assassination of Amnon, the Eldest Son of David, by His Third Eldest Son Absalom—circa 1000 B.C.

Amnon (אַמְנוֹן, *amnon, am´non*; Heb., "faithful"[49] or "steadfast"[50]), the first son of David, was assassinated in a revenge killing by

46. Chris Stevens, "Ish-Bosheth, Son of Saul," *The Lexham Bible Dictionary* (Bellingham, WA: Lexham Press, 2016).

47. Chris Stevens, "Ish-Bosheth, Son of Saul," *The Lexham Bible Dictionary* (Bellingham, WA: Lexham Press, 2016).

48. Chris Stevens, "Ish-Bosheth, Son of Saul," *The Lexham Bible Dictionary* (Bellingham, WA: Lexham Press, 2016).

49. Mark Allan Powell, "Amnon," in *The HarperCollins Bible Dictionary (Revised and Updated)*, ed. Mark Allan Powell (New York: HarperCollins, 2011), 27.

50. Isidore Singer, ed., in *The Jewish Encyclopedia: A Descriptive Record of the History, Religion, Literature, and Customs of the Jewish People from the Earliest Times to the Present Day, 12 Volumes* (New York; London: Funk & Wagnalls,

the third son of David, Absalom, because of the rape of Tamar (2 Samuel 13), Absalom's full-blooded biological sister and Amnon's half-sister. J.F. Stenning observes in 2 Sam. 13:20 that Amnon is called diminutive Aminon (אֲמִינוֹן) by Absalom, "supposed by many (on the analogy of Arabic) to be a diminutive form, purposely used by Absalom to express contempt."[51] Amnon's mother was Ahinoam, a woman from the town of Jezreel, who became one of David's early wives as per 1 Sam. 25:43; 27:3; 30:5; 2 Sam. 2:2; 3:2; 1 Chron. 3:1). Escaping and evading the murderous pursuit of the envious King Saul, David married her along with Abigail, the widow of Nabal (1 Sam. 25:43), and accompanied him to the Philistine-occupied Gath during David's early mercenary service to Achish, the Philistine King of Gath, during his forced exile from Saul's territory (1 Sam. 27:3). While in nearby Ziklag, a lightning-like Amalekite raid succeeded in taking both Ahinoam and Abigail captive while David was joining the Philistine troops mustering in battle array against Saul's forces at Aphek (1 Sam. 30:5). The Amalekites may have sought revenge against any Israelite, whether in exile or under Saul's command and control, retaliating against Saul's attempt to eliminate them in 1 Samuel 15[52] and especially targeting the province of whom they would have likely heard was Saul's heir-apparent after Samuel anointed David. David's defeat of the Amalekites emphasized his ability to serve as God's earthly vice-regent and military commander, while providing him with a convenient alibi for his whereabouts as Saul died on the battlefield at Gilboa.[53] Ahinoam bore David his first child, Amnon, after David had terminated his service to Achish of Gath and had moved

---

1901–1906), 525.

51. John F. Stenning, "AMNON," in *A Dictionary of the Bible: Dealing with Its Language, Literature, and Contents Including the Biblical Theology*, ed. James Hastings et al. (New York; Edinburgh: Charles Scribner's Sons; T. & T. Clark, 1911–1912), 83.

52. David M. Gunn, *The Fate of King Saul: An Interpretation of a Biblical Story*, JSOT Supplement Series 14 (Sheffield: JSOT Press, 1980), 110.

53. Diana V. Edelman, "Ahinoam (Person)," *Anchor Yale Bible Dictionary*, vol. 1 (New York: Doubleday, 1992), 118.

from the Philistine town of Ziklag to Hebron (2 Sam. 2:2; 3:2; 1 Chron. 3:1).[54]

Amnon [ironically meaning, Heb. *'amnôn*, 'faithful'], the eldest son of David, by Ahinoam of Jezreel (2 Sam. 3:2), was, in bitter irony, the crown prince and heir presumptive to the throne, whose prurient, sociopathic, and rapist animus is a dark vice in incisive contrast to the sterling virtues of one who would rule ("he that ruleth over men must be just," 2 Sam. 23:3). Because of the outrageous rape of his sister Tamar followed by her outrageous rejection, Absalom, the third eldest son of David, "doubly hated" Amnon—not only because of the sexual sin and shaming of Tamar but because of his ambition, coveting Amnon's position as the firstborn (2 Sam. 3:2; 13:1ff; 1 Chron. 3:1).[55] Amnon's rape of Tamar was another major incident that showed the dysfunction of David's family.[56] Amnon's father, though the "man after God's own

54. Diana V. Edelman, "Ahinoam (Person)," *Anchor Yale Bible Dictionary*, vol. 1 (New York: Doubleday, 1992), 118. "It has been proposed that the two Ahinoams were the same individual on the basis of Nathan's comment to David that Yahweh had given him "his master's wives" in 2 Sam 12:8 (Levenson 1978: 27). Such a presumption would require David to have run off with the queen mother while Saul was still on the throne, which seems unlikely. In view of the possession of the royal harem as a claim to royal legitimacy (see "Abner"), Nathan's comment can be related to David's eventual possession of Saul's wives after he ascended the throne in the wake of Eshbaal's death. Nathan refers to David's possession of more than a single wife of Saul's in v 23, which precludes the application of the phrase to Ahinoam alone. It is likely that the Jezreel that was Ahinoam's home was the town in S Judah, rather than the town in the Jezreel Valley. In his bid to build a rival state to Saul's in the hills of Judah, it would have been expedient for David to have wed the daughter of an important member of the community of Jezreel in the vicinity of Carmel (Josh 15:55, 56; Kh. Tewana?), an area with established viticulture that could offer David a possible economic base for his political growth (see DAVID)." Diana V. Edelman, "Ahinoam (Person)," *AYBD*, 1:118.

55. Geoffrey W. Bromiley, ed., "Amnon," in *The International Standard Bible Encyclopedia, Revised* (Wm. B. Eerdmans, 1979–1988), 112.

56. Richard R. Losch, in *All the People in the Bible: An A–Z Guide to the Saints, Scoundrels, and Other Characters in Scripture* (Grand Rapids, Mich.; Cambridge, U.K.: William B. Eerdmans Publishing Company, 2008), 29–30: "David's first wife, Michal, was Saul's daughter, and she had been taken from him by Saul. Although she originally had loved David, when he later forcibly brought her back she showed nothing but contempt for him. Shortly before Amnon's rape

heart," committed adultery with Bathsheba, attempted to cover the sin, then arranged for the murder of her husband Uriah the Hittite. Amnon acted with utter contempt to dehumanize, dishonoring his half-sister Tamar, counting her chastity[57] as nothing, and was, on that account, later slain by her brother Absalom (2 Sam. 3:2; 13:1f.).[58]

Absalom's [Heb *'abšālōm* (אַבְשָׁלֹם) var. Abishalom] mother was a foreigner, Maacah, daughter of Talmai, King of Geshur (2 Sam. 3:3; 1 Chron. 3:2). Geshur was a small Aramean city-state between Bashan and Hermon, which served as a buffer between Israel and Aram. David married Maacah, daughter of the king of Geshur, who became mother of Absalom (2 Sam. 3:3), which caused the two lands to be on friendly terms. Absalom would later retreat to his mother's homeland (2 Sam. 13:37–38).[59] Absalom was the third son of David, one of those born to David at Hebron by six different wives. King David had six sons in Hebron: Amnon, David's first son, by Ahinoam; Daniel, David's second son, by Abigail; Absalom, David's third and favorite son, by Maachah; Adonijah, David's son by Haggith; Shephatiah, David's son by Abital; and Ithream, David's son by Eglah. David also had four sons with Bathsheba: Shammua, Shobab, Nathan, and Solomon.

The third son, Absalom, was at the center of a long-running series of troubles that David had with his sons: he killed his older brother Amnon and later rebelled against David himself.[60] Absalom first appears on the stage of the Hebrew Bible in the tragic saga

---

of Tamar, David had committed adultery with Bathsheba and had arranged for the murder of her husband Uriah the Hittite."

57. Philip Schaff, ed., in *A Dictionary of the Bible: Including Biography, Natural History, Geography, Topography, Archæology, and Literature* (Philadelphia; New York; Chicago: American Sunday-School Union, 1880), 47.

58. James Hastings et al., in *Dictionary of the Bible* (New York: Charles Scribner's Sons, 1909), 27.

59. Chad Brand et al., eds., "Geshur," in *Holman Illustrated Bible Dictionary* (Nashville, TN: Holman Bible Publishers, 2003), 641.

60. David M. Howard Jr., "Absalom (Person)," in *The Anchor Yale Bible Dictionary*, ed. David Noel Freedman (New York: Doubleday, 1992), 45.

of Amnon's rape of their sister Tamar (2 Samuel 13). Amnon's obsessive[61] desire for and objectification/dehumanization of Tamar is depicted in 2 Samuel 13. Amnon "fell in love with her" (13:1, or rather into "obsessive"[62] lust). Acting on the perverse, deceitful advice of his cousin Jonadab, he pretended to be ill and duped his father David to let Tamar attend his needs while supposedly ill. He raped her when they were alone, then afterward "was seized with a very great loathing for her" (13:15) and threw her out in the street. After the ghastly deception and violation, Amnon's prurience turned to contempt for the object of his psychopathology, and he narcissistically banished her like an expelled, branded outcast.[63]

Absalom, justifiably infuriated, waited in cold calculation for his revenge. After two years had passed, Absalom arranged with his retainers for the murder of Amnon, which precipitated the political rift between David and Absalom, culminating in a coup de tat. David's failure to punish Amnon, as well as his affair with Bathsheba, undoubtedly contributed to Absalom's hatred of his father, which ultimately led to his rebellion and his own ignominious demise.[64]

Amnon lured, isolated, trapped, seized, and raped Tamar at the cunning, crafty suggestion of Jonadab, who told him to pretend to be ill, and ask for private care by the young, unsuspecting Tamar. [65] He forced her, despite her reasonable protestations (even offering to be given willingly in marriage by the King's command), then sent her away in disgrace, whereupon her older brother Absalom took her, "albatrossed" and "Scarlet lettered," into his

61. Keith L. Eades, "Amnon," in *Eerdmans Dictionary of the Bible*, ed. David Noel Freedman, 1st ed. (Grand Rapids: Eerdmans, 2000), 54.

62. Keith L. Eades, "Amnon," *Eerdmans Dictionary of the Bible*, 54.

63. Richard R. Losch, in *All the People in the Bible: An A–Z Guide to the Saints, Scoundrels, and Other Characters in Scripture* (Grand Rapids, Mich.; Cambridge, U.K.: William B. Eerdmans Publishing Company, 2008), 29–30.

64. Richard R. Losch, in *All the People in the Bible: An A–Z Guide to the Saints, Scoundrels, and Other Characters in Scripture* (Grand Rapids, Mich.; Cambridge, U.K.: William B. Eerdmans Publishing Company, 2008), 29–30.

65. John D. Barry et al., eds., "Amnon, Son of David," in *The Lexham Bible Dictionary* (Bellingham, WA: Lexham Press, 2016).

protective care and custody.[66] Her personal pain and public shame no doubt fueled Absalom's resolve to avenge his sister's tragic destiny, a life sentence of shame as rejected pariah. Her retort to her rapist, before consummating his *mens rea,* was a just verdict. "And I, whither shall I cause my shame to go? and as for thee, thou shalt be as one of the fools in Israel. Now therefore, I pray thee, speak unto the king; for he will not withhold me from thee."[67] Tamar's recoil and pleading that he speak to their father about marriage fell upon deaf ears, as the only sound Amnon could hear in his heart was the voice of his hormones. [68] He "seized" [69] her, then sexually assaulted her, heartlessly, then narcissistically banished her out of his abode, to which he previously cajoled her in a web of crass deceit that even suborned their own unwitting father. When she pleaded that he not add to the wrong he had already done to her,[70] Amnon added evil upon evil—shaming her person in vulgar violation, he subsequently proudly ordered her thrown into the street as rubbish. What exact effect upon Amnon's apparently psychopathically inclined psyche the stimulus of David's adultery and murder may have had is a matter for conjecture. David acted, rashly, upon his prurient impulses. His eldest son, sometime thereafter, acted upon his—like father, like son? His father murdered to cover the acts of his prurient inclinations; the son socially murdered his victim after his acts of his prurient inclinations. Never and nonetheless, Amnon is responsible for his own decisions. His dehumanization of Tamar his half-sister was so extreme, he first utilized her as a tool for self-gratification, then when through with his acquired tool, tossed her out and away as piece of trash, to be the untouchable rubbish of society.

66. John D. Barry et al., eds., "Amnon, Son of David," in *The Lexham Bible Dictionary* (Bellingham, WA: Lexham Press, 2016).

67. 2 Sam 13:13 KJV.

68. Keith L. Eades, "Amnon," in *Eerdmans Dictionary of the Bible,* ed. David Noel Freedman, 1st ed. (Grand Rapids: Wm. B. Eerdmans, 2000), 54.

69. Keith L. Eades, "Amnon," in *Eerdmans Dictionary of the Bible,* ed. David Noel Freedman, 1st ed. (Grand Rapids: Wm. B. Eerdmans, 2000), 54.

70. Keith L. Eades, "Amnon," in *Eerdmans Dictionary of the Bible,* ed. David Noel Freedman, 1st ed. (Grand Rapids: Wm. B. Eerdmans, 2000), 54.

What a contrast, in general, between his father, the "man after God's own heart" and the firstborn son, who, in general as far as the Hebrew record is concerned, was flagrantly a man after his own body's hormones. After the gruesome rape was committed, Absalom hated Amnon (13:22) with even greater hatred that the latter had shown for Tamar (13:15–19) after he satisfied his pathological lust, and he bided his time, nurturing his scheme for revenge.[71] After two years of nurturing, and concealing, his hatred, Absalom was able to lure Amnon, who himself had lured his sister into a trap. Surreptitiously, Absalom lured by subterfuge "all the king's sons" to festivities at Baal-hazor, near Ephraim, during the time of sheepshearing feast (2 Sam. 13:23–29).[72] He invited the king and princes to celebrate the shearing of his flocks at Baal-hazor.[73] While was carousing at a sheep-shearing festival, Absalom finally had his long-desired opportunity in the midst of Amnon's self-indulgent revelry.[74] Absalom acquired his long-nurtured revenge and had his servants kill Amnon, while the brothers fled for their safety. Absalom invited Amnon and the rest of David's sons to the sheepshearing festival, and at Absalom's command, the servants killed Amnon when he was drunk with wine (2 Sam 13:1–29).[75] David first mourned the death of Amnon, and then he mourned the absence of Absalom, who had fled to his mother's household

71. David M. Howard Jr., "Absalom (Person)," in *The Anchor Yale Bible Dictionary*, ed. David Noel Freedman (New York: Doubleday, 1992), 45.

72. Isidore Singer, ed., in *The Jewish Encyclopedia: A Descriptive Record of the History, Religion, Literature, and Customs of the Jewish People from the Earliest Times to the Present Day, 12 Volumes* (New York; London: Funk & Wagnalls, 1901–1906), 525.

73. Keith L. Eades, "Amnon," in *Eerdmans Dictionary of the Bible*, ed. David Noel Freedman, 1st ed. (Grand Rapids: Wm. B. Eerdmans, 2000), 54.

74. Richard R. Losch, in *All the People in the Bible: An A–Z Guide to the Saints, Scoundrels, and Other Characters in Scripture* (Grand Rapids, MI; Cambridge, U.K.: William B. Eerdmans Publishing Company, 2008), 29–30.

75. John D. Barry et al., eds., "Amnon, Son of David," in *The Lexham Bible Dictionary* (Bellingham, WA: Lexham Press, 2016).

in Geshur, where he remained for three years (13:30–39) to exist in exile.[76]

The *Jewish Encyclopedia* outlines the sage, salient commentary of Rabbinic literature upon the tragic episode of the deception, violation, and rejection of Tamar[77]:

> The sages of the Mishnah point out that Amnon's love for Tamar, his half-sister, did not arise from true affection, but from passion and lust, on which account, after having attained his desire, he immediately "hated her exceedingly." "All love which depends upon some particular thing ceases when that thing ceases; thus was the love of Amnon for Tamar" (Ab. v. 16). Amnon's love for Tamar was not, however, such a transgression as is usually supposed: for, although she was a daughter of David, her mother was a prisoner of war, who had not yet become a Jewess; consequently, Tamar also had not entered the Jewish community (Sanh. 21a). The incident of Amnon and Tamar was utilized by the sages as affording justification for their rule that a man must on no account remain alone in the company of a woman, not even of an unmarried one (Sanh. *l.c. et seq.*).[78]

Whether the implication of various Rabbis that Amnon may have viewed his half-sister as an object of his gratification, and then an item as trash to be tossed, because her mother was not biologically of the seed of Jacob, is less than questionable. Tamar was the offspring of his father, and the Fifth Commandment, as well as the Seventh, was blatantly violated by Amnon's outrageous crime, as

---

76. David M. Howard Jr., "Absalom (Person)," in *The Anchor Yale Bible Dictionary*, ed. David Noel Freedman (New York: Doubleday, 1992), 45.

77. Isidore Singer, ed., in *The Jewish Encyclopedia: A Descriptive Record of the History, Religion, Literature, and Customs of the Jewish People from the Earliest Times to the Present Day*, 12 Volumes (New York; London: Funk & Wagnalls, 1901–1906), 525.

78. Isidore Singer, ed., in *The Jewish Encyclopedia: A Descriptive Record of the History, Religion, Literature, and Customs of the Jewish People from the Earliest Times to the Present Day*, 12 Volumes (New York; London: Funk & Wagnalls, 1901–1906), 525.

well as sin, which ranked him "lowest of the low" in the annals of shame in the Hebrew Bible.[79]

The Assassination of Amasa by Joab, Both Nephews of David—circa 1000 B.C.

Amasa, a nephew of David (2 Sam. 19:14; Eng 19:13), is yet another tragic figure on the stage of the Hebrew Bible's narrations of political intrigue culminating in assassination. Amasa (עֲמָשָׂא, Hebrew 'burden' or 'burden bearer'), was the son of Ithra, according to 2 Sam. 17:25, an Israelite, but according to 1 Chron. 2:17, Jether the Ishmaelite.[80] His mother was Abigail, a sister of king David; hence he was a biological nephew of David, as Joab, his murderer, also was. Some question textual transmission regarding the name "Abigail":

> However, this latter name may be a textual corruption from 2 Sam 17:27, because Abigail is also identified as the sister of Joab's mother Zeruiah. According to 1 Chr 1:16–17, both these women were sisters of David and presumably daughters of Jesse. It has been alternately suggested that Abigail was David's half-sister and not Jesse's daughter. The wording of 2 Sam 17:25 suggests that there was something unusual or irregular about Abigail's marital relationship with Ithra.[81]

The first appearance of Amasa in the Hebrew Bible is in the rebellion of Absalom (2 Sam. 17:25), who made Amasa commander of his army. Joab, however, at the head of the King David's troops, completely routed Absalom in the forest of Ephraim (2 Sam. 18:6–8), where Absalom died an ignominious death, his head

79. Richard R. Losch, in *All the People in the Bible: An A–Z Guide to the Saints, Scoundrels, and Other Characters in Scripture* (Grand Rapids, MI; Cambridge, U.K.: William B. Eerdmans Publishing Company, 2008), 29–30.

80. Richard D. Nelson, "Amasa (Person)," in *The Anchor Yale Bible Dictionary*, ed. David Noel Freedman (New York: Doubleday, 1992), 182.

81. Richard D. Nelson, "Amasa (Person)," in *The Anchor Yale Bible Dictionary*, ed. David Noel Freedman (New York: Doubleday, 1992), 182.

replete with lengthy flowing locks, caught in branches which left him an easy shot for Joab's arrows. In the interest of national unity, and restoring federal power, David pardoned Amasa, and further, gave him the command of the army, replacing the choleric Joab (2 Sam. 19:13). As high-ranking Judahites had sided against David, including the highly esteemed Athihophel, appointing the head of formerly enemy forces was an amalgamation, allowing a mending of the fabric of David's federal rule over all Israel:

> The appointment of Amasa was one factor in David's successful appeal to his fellow Judahites (2 Sam. 19:12–15—Eng 19:11–14). David's tilt to Judah seems to have precipitated Sheba's subsequent rebellion.[82]

When Amasa came to lead the federal forces against the rebel Sheba and his rebel host, he was treacherously slain by Joab at "the great stone of Gibeon" (2 Sam. 20:8–13),[83] where Joab approached him under false pretenses as if to salute, deceitfully. In his last words to his son Solomon, David counseled that Joab's sins and crimes were such that he should suffer capital punishment (2 Kings 2:1–9).

As to the "Thirty" of the top tier of David's troops, Amasa has sometimes been identified with Amasai (Heb ʿămāśay), the chief of the "Thirty" (1 Chron. 12:19—Eng 12:18), who pledged loyalty to David when Saul was hunting for him as David fled. As Richard D. Nelson correctly observes, "There is no solid evidence either for or against this proposal."[84]

Apparently, Amasa either was unable, or simply failed, to fulfill the David's order to muster the militia of Judah in three days to meet the crisis of Sheba's resistance and rebellion (2 Sam.

---

82. Richard D. Nelson, "Amasa (Person)," in *The Anchor Yale Bible Dictionary*, ed. David Noel Freedman (New York: Doubleday, 1992). 182.

83. Robert Masson Boyd, "AMASA," in *A Dictionary of the Bible: Dealing with Its Language, Literature, and Contents Including the Biblical Theology*, ed. James Hastings et al. (New York; Edinburgh: Charles Scribner's Sons; T. & T. Clark, 1911–1912). 79.

84. Richard D. Nelson, "Amasa (Person)," in *The Anchor Yale Bible Dictionary*, ed. David Noel Freedman (New York: Doubleday, 1992). 182.

20:4–5). Time may have been a factor, as three days with necessary organization and travel time may have insufficient. Or, Amasa may have adjudged, militarily, that attacking the forces of Israel with the militia of Judah was premature, or even unwise. David's professional troops set out alone, however, among them their leader Joab (2 Sam. 20:6–7), where at the "stone of Gibeon" Joab approached Amasa in premeditation and with trickery. Amasa delayed beyond the set time, so David sent Abishai, brother of Joab, and a body of armed men after Sheba. Amasa joined forces with Abishai at "the great rock in Gibeon," where Joab, in feigned greeting, "took Amasa by the beard with his right hand to kiss him" and ran him through with his sword (20:8–10).[85] Amasa encountered them at Gibeon and was treacherously stabbed by Joab, who immediately took back effective control of the forces, replacing Amasa his cousin forthwith (vv 8–11). Efficiency is essential in a military crisis under time constraints. As time was of the essence, the sight of Amasa's corpse was not permitted to hinder the army's ongoing progress (vv 12–13). Amasa's treacherous murder would later prompt David to advise the liquidation of Joab for capital murder upon Solomon's accession (1 Kings 2:5, 32).[86]

David, the man "after God's own heart," was not without flaw—the text may imply that David's offer to Amasa was an error in political judgment (for other examples, see 2 Sam. 13:21; 18:5; 19:2–4—Eng 19:1–3; 19:42–44—Eng 41–43; 1 Kings 1:6). [87] But despite David's heart for God, his family's dynamics are replete with the dark and dismal marks of depravity, which could make one despair.

---

85. J. D. Douglas and Merrill Chapin Tenney, in *New International Bible Dictionary* (Grand Rapids, MI: Zondervan, 1987), 38.

86. Richard D. Nelson, "Amasa (Person)," in *The Anchor Yale Bible Dictionary*, ed. David Noel Freedman (New York: Doubleday, 1992) 182.

87. Richard D. Nelson, "Amasa (Person)," in *The Anchor Yale Bible Dictionary*, ed. David Noel Freedman (New York: Doubleday, 1992) 182.

The Assassinations by Athaliah Followed by the Assassination of Athaliah—circa 841–835 B.C.

Athaliah protrudes in the fabric of history of Hebrew politics as the only mass assassin who met the fate she meted out against innocent political victims. She was a significant figure in the history of Judah, being the only woman to ever reign as queen over the kingdom.[88] She was the daughter of King Ahab of Israel and likely Jezebel, making her the granddaughter of Omri.[89] Athaliah became the wife of King Jehoram of Judah and mother to King Ahaziah.[90] After Ahaziah's death, Athaliah seized power by murdering her grandchildren, except for young Joash, who was hidden by Jehosheba, Ahaziah's sister and wife of the high priest Jehoiada.[91] Athaliah ruled for six years (842–836 B.C.) and promoted the cult of Baal Melqart.[92] Her reign ended dramatically when Jehoiada orchestrated a conspiracy, revealing the hidden Joash and having Athaliah executed outside the temple.[93]

Athaliah is initially called the daughter of Omri (2 Kings 8:26; 2 Chron. 22:2), although later called the daughter of Ahab (2 Kings 8:18; 2 Chron. 21:6). Cogan and Tadmor argue that

88. Allen C. Myers, in *The Eerdmans Bible Dictionary* (Grand Rapids, MI: Eerdmans, 1987), 103l J. D. Douglas and Merrill Chapin Tenney, in *New International Bible Dictionary* (Grand Rapids, MI: Zondervan, 1987), 107–108.

89. Allen C. Myers, in *The Eerdmans Bible Dictionary* (Grand Rapids, MI: Eerdmans, 1987), 103.

90. Allen C. Myers, in *The Eerdmans Bible Dictionary* (Grand Rapids, MI: Eerdmans, 1987), 103.

91. Allen C. Myers, in *The Eerdmans Bible Dictionary* (Grand Rapids, MI: Eerdmans, 1987), 103; J. D. Douglas and Merrill Chapin Tenney, in *New International Bible Dictionary* (Grand Rapids, MI: Zondervan, 1987), 107–108; James Hastings et al., in *Dictionary of the Bible* (New York: Charles Scribner's Sons, 1909), 71.

92. Allen C. Myers, in *The Eerdmans Bible Dictionary* (Grand Rapids, MI: Eerdmans, 1987), 103.

93. Allen C. Myers, in *The Eerdmans Bible Dictionary* (Grand Rapids, MI: Eerdmans, 1987), 103; J. D. Douglas and Merrill Chapin Tenney, in *New International Bible Dictionary* (Grand Rapids, MI: Zondervan, 1987), 107–108; James Hastings et al., in *Dictionary of the Bible* (New York: Charles Scribner's Sons, 1909), 71.

Athaliah is the daughter of Ahab and the granddaughter of Omri, as "daughter" can mean "female descendant" as well as be indicative of a biological daughter.[94] Even if she was not the daughter of Jezebel, Athaliah was probably educated under the supervision of Jezebel as per Brenner and Katzenstein.[95] Katzenstein resolves ambiguities by concluding that Athaliah was the daughter of Omri mentioned in 2 Kings 8:26 and 2 Chron. 22:2, but that she grew up under Ahab—he posits she was an orphan—thus explaining "daughter of Ahab" and "house of Ahab."[96] Spanier also posits that "daughter" may refer to Ahab's protection of her,[97] just as Tamar was under the protection of her brother, Absalom.[98]

Athaliah's institution of Baal worship was extensive. Walter Brueggemann views the likely motive of Athaliah's extermination of the royal house was consolidation of power so that no Yahwist resistance could be mustered from the royal court.[99] Fretheim concurs that Athaliah likely sought a clean sweep of Yahwist nobility so as to solidify Baal worship in Judah in response to Jehu's coup in Israel.[100] Brenner claims that Athaliah proclaimed the cult as official, alongside the worship of Yahweh,[101] because of the existence

94. Mordechai Cogan and Hayim Tadmor, *II Kings: A New Translation with Introduction and Commentary*, Anchor Yale Bible Commentaries, vol 11 (New York: Doubleday, 1988), 98.

95. Athalya Brenner-Idan, *The Israelite Woman: Social Role and Literary Type in Biblical Narrative* (Sheffield: Sheffield Academic Press, 1985), 28; H.J. Katzenstein, "Who Were the Parents of Athaliah," *Israel Exploration Journal*, Vol. 5, No. 3 (1955), 194–197.

96. H.J. Katzenstein, "Who Were the Parents of Athaliah," *Israel Exploration Journal*, Vol. 5, No. 3 (1955), 197.

97. 2 Sam. 14:27; Spanier, Ktziah. "The Queen Mother in the Judaean Royal Court: Maacah—A Case Study." In *A Feminist Companion to Samuel and Kings*, edited by Athalya Brenner, 186–195. Sheffield: Sheffield Academic Press, 1994.

98. Ginny Brewer-Boydston, "Athaliah, Queen of Judah," in *The Lexham Bible Dictionary*, ed. John D. Barry et al. (Bellingham, WA: Lexham Press, 2016).

99. Walter Brueggemann, *1 & 2 Kings*, Smyth & Helwys Bible Commentary, vol. 8 (Macon: Smyth & Helwys, 2000), 407–408.

100. Terence E. Fretheim, *First and Second Kings* (Louisville: Westminster John Knox, 1999), 178.

101. Athalya Brenner-Idan, *The Israelite Woman: Social Role and Literary*

of a temple dedicated to Baal.[102] Since 922 B.C., Jeroboam, fugitive turned head of state of the seceded ten (10) northern tribes, solidified and galvanized the northern new nation with its own distorted, modified religion, as he "intended a radical religious reform that would cement the northern secession[103] . . . this act earns him repeated condemnation throughout 1 and 2 Kings (e.g., 1 Kings 14:16; 15:29–30; 16:30–31; 2 Kings 3:3; 10:29–31)."[104]

Athaliah's marriage to Jehoram appears to have been part of a treaty—or political alliance—between the seceded northern and continuing southern kingdoms.[105] Ishida hypothesizes a unification of Israel and Judah through the marriage—Jehoram and Athaliah effectively reunite the two nations into one through a common headship.[106] Marriage, a typical international means of solemnifying a peace treaty, appears to be the political means of putting an end to the political hostilities between Judah and Israel since the division of the monarchy.[107]

Miller and Hayes, in their *History of Ancient Israel and Judah*, point out that the separation of the kingdoms hampered the free flow of trade.[108] Spanier notes Omri's negotiations with Phoenicia and Judah in order to engage in commerce with them, gaining access to more remote trading partners; political marriages

---

Type in Biblical Narrative (London: T&T Clark, 2014), 29–30.

102. Ginny Brewer-Boydston, "Athaliah, Queen of Judah," in *The Lexham Bible Dictionary*, ed. John D. Barry et al. (Bellingham, WA: Lexham Press, 2016).

103. Serge Frolov, "*Days of Shiloh* in the Kingdom of Israel," *Biblica* 76, no. 2 (1995): 210–218.

104. Jin H. Han, "Divided Kingdom," in *The Lexham Bible Dictionary*, ed. John D. Barry et al. (Bellingham, WA: Lexham Press, 2016).

105. Ackerman, "Queen Mother and the Cult," 295; Spanier, "Northern Israelite Queen Mother," 141–42; Brenner, *The Israelite Woman*, 207.

106. Tomoo Ishida, *The Royal Dynasties in Ancient Israel: A Study on the Formation and Development of Royal-Dynastic Ideology*, Beihefte zur Zeitschrift für die alttestamentliche Wissenschaft 142 (Berlin: W. de Gruyter, 1977), 159. (degruyter.com)

107. Ackerman, "Queen Mother and the Cult," 295; Spanier, "Northern Israelite Queen Mother," 141–42; Brenner, *The Israelite Woman*, 207.

108. Miller and Hayes, *History of Ancient Israel and Judah*, 267.

consummated these treaties and alliances.[109] Ishida hypothesizes a unification of Israel and Judah through the marriage facilitated not only a cessation of internecine warfare but free commerce. Jehoram and Athaliah establish their reign in full cooperation with the House of Omri.[110] After Jehoram's death, his son with Athaliah continues the alliance. Athaliah may have usurped the throne to continue the reign of the House of Omri/Ahab as part of the treaty made between Israel and Judah.[111]

Athaliah's death is the end of permanent eradication of Yahwism via replacement with Baalism. Her assassination is a vivid, dramatic descent—"And when she looked, behold, the king stood by a pillar, as the manner *was*, and the princes and the trumpeters by the king, and all the people of the land rejoiced, and blew with trumpets: and Athaliah rent her clothes, and cried, Treason, Treason. But Jehoiada the priest commanded the captains of the hundreds, the officers of the host, and said unto them, Have her forth without the ranges: and him that followeth her kill with the sword. For the priest had said, Let her not be slain in the house of the LORD. And they laid hands on her; and she went by the way by the which the horses came into the king's house: and there was she slain" (2 Kings 11:14–16).

The Assassination of Joash/Jehoash—circa B.C. 835–796 B.C.

The reign of Joash, also called Jehoash, the ninth king of Judah, signifies vividly the principle that we become like those around us—our mentors make us or break us. Although Jehoash "did what was right in the eyes of the Lord" for a time, there were problems

109. Spanier, "Queen Mother in the Judaean Royal Court," 79.

110. Tomoo Ishida, *The Royal Dynasties in Ancient Israel: A Study on the Formation and Development of Royal-Dynastic Ideology*, Beihefte zur Zeitschrift für die alttestamentliche Wissenschaft 142 (Berlin: W. de Gruyter, 1977), 159. (degruyter.com)

111. Ginny Brewer-Boydston, "Athaliah, Queen of Judah," in *The Lexham Bible Dictionary*, ed. John D. Barry et al. (Bellingham, WA: Lexham Press, 2016).

during his reign. It is evident that he did not tear down the places of idolatry throughout Judah (2 Kings 12:3) and that his reign ended tragically after Jehoiada died (2 Chron. 24:17–19).[112]

The account of Jehoash in 2 Kings ends abruptly after he pays tribute to Hazael, king of Aram (2 Kings 12:17–18). Yet the Chronicler continues the narrative to include the tragic ruin of Jehoash's reign. After Jehoiada died, Jehoash began listening to idolaters and turned away from Yahweh. God sent Zechariah, the son of Jehoiada, to pronounce His judgment upon Jehoash. Unwilling to repent, Jehoash commanded Zechariah to be killed by stoning in the courtyard of the temple. [113]

Jehoash, a classic tragic figure, died in the aftermath of a Syrian military campaign that left him wounded (2 Chron. 24:23–25), whereupon his servants, avenging his cruelty to Zechariah the priest, entered his bedroom and assassinated him on his bed (2 Chron. 24:25), apparently while asleep, thus terminating his degenerating reign. Although Jehoash rose and ascended as the Davidic legitimate heir, he descended and died in disgrace. Daniel J. Thorpe observes that Chronicles presents his promising rise and tragic fall in the rhetorical form inclusio. His story begins when his aunt spares him from Athaliah's wrath while hiding him in a bedroom (2 Chron. 22:11), securing him for posterity in the Temple. His saga culminates with his closest, nearest officials assassinating him on his own, wrongfully deemed safe and secure, bed (2 Chron. 24:25).[114]

112. Daniel J. Thorpe, "Jehoash, King of Judah," in *The Lexham Bible Dictionary*, ed. John D. Barry et al. (Bellingham, WA: Lexham Press, 2016).

113. Daniel J. Thorpe, "Jehoash, King of Judah," in *The Lexham Bible Dictionary*, ed. John D. Barry et al. (Bellingham, WA: Lexham Press, 2016).

114. Daniel J. Thorpe, "Jehoash, King of Judah," in *The Lexham Bible Dictionary*, ed. John D. Barry et al. (Bellingham, WA: Lexham Press, 2016).

Sennacherib, King of Assyria (704–681 B.C.) Assassinated by His Own Sons While Worshiping His Deity Nisroch

A dramatic episode in the history of assassinations crescendos and climaxes in 2 Kings 19:37 with the ignominious death of Sennacherib, King of Assyria (704–681 B.C.): "And it came to pass, as he was worshipping in the house of Nisroch his god, that Adrammelech and Sharezer his sons smote him with the sword: and they escaped into the land of Armenia. And Esarhaddon his son reigned in his stead."[115] The designation Sennacherib is an Assyrian royal name meaning "Sin (the god) has replaced my brother." The treachery of Sennacherib's assassination protrudes because he is murdered by his own offspring, Adrammelech and Sharezer. Adrammelech, both divine and personal name meaning "Adra is king," may be based on an earlier form Hadadmelech, "Hadad is king," using the name of a Canaanite deity. Sharezer, one of the two sons of Sennacherib who murdered the Assyrian king (2 Kings 19:37 = Isa. 37:38), with his brother (likely older) Adrammelech, plunged the Assyrian empire into a brief dynastic crisis until the youngest son, Esarhaddon, returned from exile and assumed the throne in 680 B.C. Only Scripture records the names of the familial assassins—there is no Mesopotamian source for the names of these sons, although the murder of Sennacherib at the hand of his own sons is historical.[116] Based on the construction of Akkadian names, Sharezer here is only a partial name ("[The God X] protect the king" = *šar-uṣur*), and a divine name should be included (e.g., Nebu, thus Nebusharezer).[117]

---

115. *The Holy Bible: King James Version*, Electronic Edition of the 1900 Authorized Version. (Bellingham, WA: Logos Research Systems, Inc., 2009), 2 Kings 19:37.

116. Nabonidus inscription, *Ancient Near Eastern Texts Relating to the Old Testament*, 3rd ed., ed. James B. Pritchard (Princeton: Princeton University Press, 1969), 309.

117. Daniel L. Smith-Christopher, "Sharezer," in *Eerdmans Dictionary of the Bible*, ed. David Noel Freedman, Allen C. Myers, and Astrid B. Beck (Grand Rapids, MI: W.B. Eerdmans, 2000), 1197.

One reading of the Hebrew manuscripts describes this Adrammelech as Sennacherib's son (KJV, NIV, RSV)[118] during his worship in the temple of Nisroch (2 Kings 19:37).[119] The name of the deity "Nisroch" is elusive (2 Kings 19:37; Isa. 37:38)—no deity of this name is otherwise known, although it is perhaps a corruption of the name Marduk,[120] Nusku (the fire god),[121] or Ashur.[122] Also, "Nisroch" may be an adaption from early Greek readings "Esdrach" and "Asorach."[123] Sennacherib's power play and international duel with Tirhakah, the Egyptian pharaoh of the 25th Dynasty (689–664 B.C.) who supported Hezekiah's revolt against Sennacherib (2 Kings 19:8–9; Isa. 37:9),[124] ended ignominiously with Sennacherib's strategic route and unsuspected murder at the hands of his own sons. The Babylonian Chronicles, unlike Isaiah, recount the murder of Sennacherib, though the assassins are not

118. Chad Brand et al., eds., "Adrammelech," in *Holman Illustrated Bible Dictionary* (Nashville, TN: Holman Bible Publishers, 2003), 30.

119. Chad Brand et al., eds., "Adrammelech," in *Holman Illustrated Bible Dictionary* (Nashville, TN: Holman Bible Publishers, 2003), 30.

120. "Chief god of Babylon, sometimes called Merodach or Bel, the Babylonian equivalent of Baal meaning "lord." He was credited with creation, a feat reenacted each new year and celebrated with a festival. In typical ancient Near Eastern fashion, Marduk was proclaimed king." Chad Brand et al., eds., "Marduk," in *Holman Illustrated Bible Dictionary* (Nashville, TN: Holman Bible Publishers, 2003), 1076.

121. "According to one of the articles, Nuzku was a servant of the god Bel in ancient Assyrian mythology. During a lunar eclipse, which was believed to be caused by seven evil spirits attacking the moon-god, Bel sent Nuzku as his messenger to the Ocean Deep. Nuzku's task was to convey Bel's message to Ea, another deity residing in the Ocean Deep, presumably to seek counsel against these malevolent spirits." Louis H. Gray et al., "Demons and Spirits," in *Encyclopædia of Religion and Ethics*, ed. James Hastings, John A. Selbie, and Louis H. Gray (Edinburgh; New York: T. & T. Clark; Charles Scribner's Sons, 1908–1926), 570.

122. Chad Brand et al., eds., "Nisroch," in *Holman Illustrated Bible Dictionary* (Nashville, TN: Holman Bible Publishers, 2003), 1194.

123. Chad Brand et al., eds., "Nisroch," in *Holman Illustrated Bible Dictionary* (Nashville, TN: Holman Bible Publishers, 2003), 1194.

124. Chad Brand et al., eds., "Tirhakah," in *Holman Illustrated Bible Dictionary* (Nashville, TN: Holman Bible Publishers, 2003), 1600.

identified. Isaiah, however, identities the assassins—Adrammelech and Sharezer, two of his sons (Isa. 37:36–38). Sennacherib's campaign, although successful up to the point of siege and conquest of nearby Lachish, failed in its siege of Jerusalem due to divine intervention (cf. 2 Kings 19:8–36; 2 Chron. 32:20–32; Isa. 37:8–37).[125]

The ironic assassination of Sennacherib underscores the Sisyphean tragedy of the rise of a pompous conqueror, who can boast that he "shut up Hezekiah as a bird in a cage" but retreats strategically in defeat, only to be murdered by his own two sons in the place of worship of his god. "Pride goeth before destruction, And an haughty spirit before a fall" (Prov. 16:18); not all epic tragedies are Greek.

Amaziah (796–767 B.C.)

King Amaziah of Judah struck down his father's assassins—Jehozabad and Zabad—as per 2 Kings 14.5–6:

> And it came to pass, as soon as the kingdom was confirmed in his hand, that he slew his servants which had slain the king his father. 6 But the children of the murderers he slew not: according unto that which is written in the book of the law of Moses, wherein the Lord commanded, saying, The fathers shall not be put to death for the children, nor the children be put to death for the

---

125. Much debate and disputation has transpired over dates of Sennacherib's invasion of Judah. Elizabeth Loftus illustrates difficulties in ascertaining accuracy: "But there is a hitch. As we put meat and muscles on the bare bones of the happening-truth, we can be caught up—captured, if you will—within our own stories. We become confused about where the happening-truth leaves us off and the story-truth begins, because the story-truth, which is so much more vivid, detailed and *real* than the happening-truth, becomes our reality." E.R. Loftus and K. Ketcham, *The Myth of Repressed Memory* (New York: St. Martin's Griffin, 1994), 39. For consideration of the issues of chronology of the invasion of Judah by Sennacherib, see Bob Becking, "Chronology: A Skeleton without Flesh? Sennacherib's Campaign as a Case-Study," in *"Like a Bird in a Cage": The Invasion of Sennacherib in 701 Bce*, ed. Lester L. Grabbe, vol. 363 of *Journal for the Study of the Old Testament Supplement Series* (London; New York: T&T Clark, 2003).

fathers; but every man shall be put to death for his own sin.[126]

2 Kings underscores that Amaziah showed restraint in the punishment of his father's assassins, by not executing capital punishment against the assassins' children and families. As the *Anchor Commentary* notes in regard to the ancient Near Eastern pattern of "blood revenge":

> The practice of blood revenge was common in the ancient Near East and persists in certain traditional societies of the modern Near East. The avenger is duty-bound to slay the murderer or one of his kinsmen, thus righting the imbalance in the community caused by the original loss. Similarly, usurpers insured their throne by exterminating the family of the former king who were potential rivals and avengers. (See M. Greenberg, s.v. "Avenger of Blood," *IBD* 1.321.) Amaziah's act in sparing the sons of his father's assassins was thus a departure from customary practice, and as such is duly stressed by the Deuteronomistic historian. His act was in line with Deuteronomic law (Deut. 24:16) quoted in the verse. From the wording of v. 6, it is unclear whether the historian meant that Amaziah actually was guided by the nucleus of the "book of the Teaching of Moses" (which must have existed at that time) . . .[127]

Although Amaziah's virtue in following Deuteronomy 24:16, not to judge the children or families of the blood-guilty, is notable, his other vices, including worshiping the gods of Edom, protrude in the Hebrew Bible as reprehensible.

126. *The Holy Bible: King James Version*, Electronic Edition of the 1900 Authorized Version. (Bellingham, WA: Logos Research Systems, Inc., 2009), 2 Kings 14:5–6.

127. Mordechai Cogan and Hayim Tadmor, *II Kings: A New Translation with Introduction and Commentary*, vol. 11 of *Anchor Yale Bible* (New Haven; London: Yale University Press, 2008), 155.

Amon (643/2–641/40 B.C.), King of Judah, Is Assassinated by His Servants, and His Servants, in Turn, Are Themselves Assassinated

In 2 Kings 21:23, a conspiracy formed to assassinate the King of Judah, Amon. The servants of King Amon forged their common cause to eliminate their principal, conspired to assassinate, and executed their king. The servants of the King, knowing his vulnerabilities, perpetrated the assassination of Amon, king of Judah, in Jerusalem. [128] After Amon's reign for only two years, the people rose up against the conspirators and executed them all, then proceeded to install Amon's eight-year-old son, Josiah, as King of Judah, as per 2 Kings 21:19–24 and 2 Chronicles 33:21–25. 2 Kings 21:24 describes a forceful response—capital punishment, in which the justice-seeking people of Judah strike down the conspirators.[129] Again, the assassins are assassinated.

As T.R. Hobbs, in the *Word Biblical Commentary* remarks: "The brief and apparently inauspicious reign of Amon is dealt with in a few sentences. His most notable achievement was to continue the policy of his father, and the most significant event of his reign was his untimely assassination." Ironically, משלמת, "Meshulemeth," a feminine form of שלמה "Solomon," is related to the root שלם "to recompense." Assassination appears to be ironic recompense to remedy assassination.[130] Hermann L. Strack and Paul Billerbeck, in *A Commentary on the New Testament from the Talmud & Midrash*, note that Rabbinic literature would later accuse Amon of an incestuous relationship with his biological mother, of course

---

128. Isaiah Hoogendyk, *All the Killings in the Bible*, Faithlife Biblical and Theological Lists (Bellingham, WA: Faithlife, 2021), 2 Ki 21:23–24.

129. Isaiah Hoogendyk, *All the Killings in the Bible*, Faithlife Biblical and Theological Lists (Bellingham, WA: Faithlife, 2021), 2 Ki 21:23–24.

130. T. R. Hobbs, *2 Kings*, vol. 13 of *Word Biblical Commentary* (Dallas: Word, Incorporated, 1985), 310. "Derivatives of the root are common in Hebrew names (Shallum, Meshullam, Absalom, Solomon, etc.), and it appears in Lachish 3:20 and 9:7."

forbidden explicitly in Leviticus 18:6–16. The Hebrew Bible, however, is silent as to this allegation.[131]

T.R. Hobbs further explores a possible wider scope for motivation for Amon's assassination, including possible international intrigue:

> Amon's ignominious end is the only event of his short reign deemed worthy of comment by the writer. Since the assassination took place within the palace, it has all the marks of a palace coup, but the reasons are nowhere stated. A. Malamat (*VTSup* 28 [1974] 126) suggests that the assassination was instigated by Egypt. Implied in the account is that Amon's death at such an untimely moment (he was thirty-two years old) was a judgment for apostasy, but other political reasons were undoubtedly present. Malamat (*VTSup* 28 [1974] 126; *IEJ* 3 [1953] 82–102; *JANESCU* 5 [1973] 268–78) suggests that the murder was for his pro-Assyrian policies, and at the instigation of Egypt (so also Reviv, *World History of the Jewish People* 4:207). Nikolsky (*ZAW* 45 [1927] 171–90, 241–53) suggests exactly the opposite. The former seems more likely, but such motivations are obviously of no concern to our writer. If Amon continued the policies of his father, which included indiscriminate and unjustified murder, that would be sufficient reason for the assassination.[132]

131. Hermann L. Strack and Paul Billerbeck, *A Commentary on the New Testament from the Talmud & Midrash*, ed. Jacob N. Cerone, trans. Joseph Longarino (Bellingham, WA: Lexham Press, 2021), 403. "King Amon in passing, stating that a later time accused him and his biological mother of incestuous intercourse. This accusation is presented in the context of discussing various forms of incest in ancient Israel, including relations with a father's wife. The article notes that such incestuous behavior is attested to in several biblical passages, including Genesis 35:22, 49:4, and 2 Samuel 16:21–22. It's important to note that the articles do not provide specific details about Amon's reign or his actions as King of Judah. For more comprehensive information about Amon as King of Judah, a different query might be necessary."

132. T. R. Hobbs, *2 Kings*, vol. 13 of *Word Biblical Commentary* (Dallas: Word, Incorporated, 1985), 310.

The author of the Hebrew Bible, however, weighs the theological reason for Amon's demise, that he did not follow in the ways of Yahweh:

> And he did *that which was* evil in the sight of the Lord, as his father Manasseh did. 21 And he walked in all the way that his father walked in, and served the idols that his father served, and worshipped them: 22 And he forsook the Lord God of his fathers, and walked not in the way of the Lord.[133]

The perspective of the Hebrew Bible on the reason for Amon's demise is spiritual, not political.

Conclusion

The tragic pattern of political assassination echoes through Scripture, underscoring the spiritual and eternal principle that the love of power may become a root of murder. Power corrupts, and absolute power, as Lord Acton coined, "corrupts absolutely." Further, envy of power may also absolutely corrupt.

In the history of the northern Kingdom of Israel, seven kings were assassinated in political intrigue:

1. Nadab (ca. 909–908 B.C.)—Assassinated by Baasha, who then took the throne (1 Kings 15:27–28);

2. Elah (ca. 886–885 B.C.)—Assassinated by Zimri, one of his commanders, while drunk (1 Kings 16:8–10);

3. Zimri (ca. 885 B.C.)—Ruled for only seven days before committing suicide by setting the palace on fire when Omri seized power (1 Kings 16:15–18);

4. Pekahiah (ca. 737–736 B.C.)—Assassinated by Pekah, one of his officers, who then took the throne (2 Kings 15:23–25);

---

133. *The Holy Bible: King James Version*, Electronic Edition of the 1900 Authorized Version. (Bellingham, WA: Logos Research Systems, Inc., 2009), 2 Ki 21:20–22.

5. Pekah (ca. 736–732 B.C.)—Assassinated by Hoshea, who became the last king of Israel (2 Kings 15:30);

6. Shallum (ca. 752 B.C.)—Ruled for just one month before being assassinated by Menahem, who then became king (2 Kings 15:10–14);

7. Zechariah (ca. 753 B.C.)—The last of Jehu's dynasty, assassinated by Shallum after a brief six-month reign (2 Kings 15:8–10).

These assassinations reflect the instability and frequent power struggles in the northern kingdom, which ultimately fell to Assyria in 722 B.C.[134]

In the history of the Kingdom of Judah, three (3) kings were assassinated, less than half of those assassinated by political intrigue in the Northen Kingdom of the ten tribes of Israel:

1. King Joash (Jehoash) (835–796 B.C.)—assassinated by his officials after being wounded in battle against the Arameans (2 Kings 12:19–21; 2 Chron. 24:25–26). [135]

2. King Amaziah (796–767 B.C.)—also assassinated by his own officials in Lachish, as per 2 Chron. 25:27–28.

3. King Amon (642–640 B.C.) —assassinated by his own servants after a brief reign of two years (2 Kings 21:23–24; 2 Chron. 33:24–25).[136]

All three were victims of internal conspiracies rather than foreign invasions. Internal instability and intrigue plagued the Southern Kingdom as did external, international power plays.

---

134. Text generated by ChatGPT, OpenAI, https://chat.openai.com.
135. Text generated by ChatGPT, OpenAI, https://chat.openai.com.
136. Text generated by ChatGPT, OpenAI, https://chat.openai.com.

BIBLICAL ANALYSIS

The Key Lexical Term for Assassin, "Σικάριος"—Biblical Lexical Exegesis and Analysis

The Hebrew Bible and the Greek New Testament are "the two lips by which God has spoken to us," said Augustine. The Greek New Testament includes a particularly salient, vivid term for assassin. Protruding in the Greek New Testament is the term σικάριος,[1] in Acts 21:38, spoken by the Roman commander interrogating Paul.[2] The Roman commanding officer mistook Paul for the insurrectionist who conflagrated an "uproar" and led out into the wilderness 4,000 men who were murderers/assassins. According to Acts 21:38 the tribune of the Roman cohort stationed in the Antonia suspected that Paul was the Egyptian who a short time before had incited 4,000 *sicarii* to rebellion and led them out into the desert. Richard I. Pervo, in *Acts: A Commentary*, Hermeneia, 21.37–40 remarks at Paul's composure, coolness, and collectedness while on the verge of excruciating torture:

1. Literally, a Sicarri, a "sica" (dagger under the garb) bearing murder, bandit, and assassin. G. Abbott-Smith, *A Manual Greek Lexicon of the New Testament* (New York: Charles Scribner's Sons, 1922), 406.

2. "...οὐκ ἄρα σὺ εἶ ὁ Αἰγύπτιος ὁ πρὸ τούτων τῶν ἡμερῶν ἀναστατώσας καὶ ἐξαγαγὼν εἰς τὴν ἔρημον τοὺς τετρακισχιλίους ἄνδρας τῶν σικαρίων;" (Acts 21:38 LXX-GNT).

On the very precipice of torture, Paul raises a polite
question that causes the tribune to make a 180-degree
turn in his character assessment. His question is best
understood as a reference to the quality of Paul's Greek
accent, since a Jewish rebel31 from Egypt was likely to
have spoken some Greek.32 Paul exhibited the fluency of
an educated native speaker, a fellow who had just disem-
barked from the train from Princeton rather than some
peasant just off the boat from Palermo. Rather more dif-
ficult to rationalize is how Claudius Lysias (for such is
his name [23:26]) was able to determine how a person
being assaulted in the vicinity of the temple was a specific
terrorist. Lysias's intelligence is bad, for his identification
confuses two very different sorts of rebels, prophetic
leaders who hoped for support from on high, and realistic assassins who struck at upper-class supporters of
Rome. Luke has drawn this medley about "the Egyptian"
and his association with "the wilderness" and "the sicarii"
from Josephus (*Bell.* 2.254–63; *Ant.* 20.161–71). It serves
no other logic than to be a splendid foil for the famous
riposte. Paul is a Jew, which qualifies him to address this
audience—and would also serve to refute claims that he
is gentile trespasser on holy ground. He is also a citizen
of Tarsus, a venerable bastion of Hellenic culture.[3]

Pervo remarks on the tribune's negligence to investigate Paul:

> The tribune's failure to investigate or verify these as-
> sertions exhibits the force of Paul's personality, which
> positively radiated refinement and gentility. Paul does
> not wear his heart on his sleeve. He says nothing about
> his Roman citizenship. For Lysias just now, Tarsus will
> do. Within thirty-five verses the following characters
> emerge: (1) victim of mob (reader's perspective), (2)
> Egyptian revolutionary terrorist (tribune's perspective),
> (3) cultivated citizen of Tarsus (tribune's perspective),
> (4) highly skilled orator (temple audience's perspec-
> tive), (5) well-educated, ardent, observant Jew (reader's
> perspective), (6) Roman citizen (soldiers' perspective).

3. Richard I. Pervo, *Acts: A Commentary*, Hermeneia 65P; eds. Harold W.
Attridge; Accordance electronic ed. (Minneapolis: Fortress Press, 2009), 553–554.

Oratorical handbooks recommended that different credentials were suitable for different audiences.35 Luke's Paul had certainly grasped that advice.[4]

The term is a Latin derivative, from the Latin *sica*, a sharp slightly curved dagger carried under clothing surreptitiously by the *Sacarri*, a band of violent bandit-assassins.[5] The *Sicarii* primarily targeted Jewish collaborators friendly to the Romans rather than the Romans themselves. The designation *sicarii* actually derived from the Romans.[6] Both Hippolytus and Origen refer to them, never in the singular, always in the plural.[7] The later Jewish and Christian referred to them as per the criminal provisions against such terrorist bands in Roman law.[8]

This term does not appear in the Greek classical period, nor does it appear in the Septuagint (LXX) or any other Greek translation of the Hebrew Bible nor the Apocrypha. The term, however, appears once in Hippolytus (c. A.D. 160–235), and once in Origin (A.D. 185–254), pupil of Clement of Alexandria,[9] but saliently

4. Richard I. Pervo, *Acts: A Commentary*, Hermeneia 65P; eds. Harold W. Attridge; Accordance electronic ed. (Minneapolis: Fortress Press, 2009), 553–554.

5. σιχάριος, -ου, ὁ (Lat.; <*sica, a dagger* carried under their clothing by the *Sicarii*), *a bandit, assassin, one of the Sicarii* (FlJ, B.J., ii, 17, 6, al.): Ac 21:38.† G. Abbott-Smith, *A Manual Greek Lexicon of the New Testament* (New York: Charles Scribner's Sons, 1922), 406.

6. The term adapts from the Roman *sica*, the short concealable sword, a favorite of assassins deploying for close assault and termination of an individual target/victim.

7. Hippolytus (c. A.D. 160–235), disciple of Irenaeus. His main work *A Refutation of All Heresies* in 10 books is directed against Greek philosophy as the mother of all heresies, ed. by different scholars in *Die griech. christi. Schriftsteller der ersten 3 Jahrhunderte*, 1897 ff. Origen, of Alexandria (A.D. 185–254), pupil of Clement of Alexandria, and most learned and fruitful representative of ancient Christian scholarship and culture, ed. by different scholars in *Die griech, christl. Schriftsteller der ersten 3 Jahrhunderte*, 1899 ff.

8. Otto Betz, "Σιχάριος," *Theological Dictionary of the New Testament* (Grand Rapids, Mich.: Eerdmans, 1964-), 278.

9. Origen, *Contra Celsum* 2.13, in *Origenes Werke*, vol. 2 of *Die griechischen christlichen Schriftsteller der ersten drei Jahrhunderte*, ed. Paul Koetschau (Leipzig: J.C. Hinrichs, 1899), 142, lines 10–22. He says the Samaritans were thought to be *sicarii* because they clung fast to circumcision. Hadrian compared this to

in the Koine (Common Post-Alexander) Greek of Josephus, the Roman-funded Jewish historian. Rabbinic literature also spoke occasionally of סִיקָרִים/ין, the Hebrew/Aramaic transliteration of Ἰωσήφ/סֵי. Josephus, the Latinized of Ἰωσήφ/יסֵ, commissioned by the Romans to record the history of Rome's "Jewish Wars" described the *sicarii* [italics added]:

> **6.** (425) Now the next day was the festival of Xylophory; upon which the custom was for every one to bring wood for the altar (that there might never be a want of fuel for that fire which was unquenchable and always burning). Upon that day they excluded the opposite party from the observation of this part of religion. And *when they had joined to themselves many of the Sicarii, who crowded in among the weaker people (that was the name for such robbers as had under their bosoms swords called Sicae), they grew bolder, and carried their undertakings further;* (426) *insomuch that the king's soldiers were overpowered by their multitude and boldness; and so they gave way, and were driven out of the upper city by force.* The others then set fire to the house of Ananias the high priest, and to the palaces of Agrippa and Bernice; (427) after which *they carried the fire to the place where the archives were reposited, and made haste to burn the contracts belonging to their creditors,* and thereby dissolve their obligations for paying their debts; and this was done, *in order to gain the multitude of those who had been debtors, and that they might persuade the poorer sort to join in their insurrection with safety against the more wealthy;* so the keepers of the records fled away, and the rest set fire to them. (428) And when they had thus burnt down the nerves of the city, they fell upon their enemies; at which time some of the men of power, and of the high priests, went into the vaults under ground, and concealed themselves, (429) while other fled with the king's soldiers to the upper palace, and shut the gates immediately; among whom were Ananias the high priest, and the ambassadors that had

---

castration, which had been forbidden since Domitian and placed under the penalties of the *lex Cornelia de sicariis et veneficis*: Roman law against murderers (sicarii) and poisoners.

been sent to Agrippa. And now the seditious were contented with the victory they had gotten, and the buildings they had burnt down, and proceeded no further.[10]

The lexicographer Barclay Newman defines the term as "terrorist, cutthroat, assassin" and a "member of a fanatical group of nationalists."[11] Hence, in context of First Century Koine (Common Post-Alexander) Greek, the term denotes a political motivation for close assault, clandestine assassinations. The lexicographer James Strong coins the term "dagger-man." a "freebooting" assassin who is a political "fanatic" justly outlawed by Roman law.[12] The lexicographers Timothy Friberg, Barbara Friberg, and Neva F. Miller add their ancillary conclusion—they see the term connoting not only a "terrorist" in general but more focused, a "cutthroat, especially" "of fanatical armed guerrilla bands hostile to foreign overlordship."[13]

Josephus described the insurrectionist band of followers of one such alpha σικάριος, which followers were deluded with his promises of "deliverance and freedom from the miseries they were under," so that the Roman commander Festus was tasked with subduing and neutralizing the entire band of terrorist-bandits [italics added]:

> And then it was *that the sicarii, as they were called, who were robbers, grew numerous. They made use of small swords, not much different in length from the Persian acinacae, but somewhat crooked, and like the Roman sicae [or sickles] as they were called; and from these weapons these robbers got their denomination; and with these weapons they slew a great many; (187) for they mingled*

10. Flavius Josephus and William Whiston, *The Works of Josephus: Complete and Unabridged* (Peabody: Hendrickson, 1987), 625.

11. Barclay M. Newman Jr., *A Concise Greek-English Dictionary of the New Testament.* (Stuttgart, Germany: Deutsche Bibelgesellschaft; United Bible Societies, 1993), 162.

12. James Strong, *The New Strong's Dictionary of Hebrew and Greek Words* (Nashville: Thomas Nelson, 1996).

13. Timothy Friberg, Barbara Friberg, and Neva F. Miller, *Analytical Lexicon of the Greek New Testament* (Grand Rapids, MI: Baker Books, 2000), 348.

themselves among the multitude at their festivals, when they were *come up in crowds from all parts to the city to worship God, as we said before, and easily slew those that they had a mind to slay.* They also came frequently upon the villages belonging to their enemies, with their weapons, and plundered them, and set them on fire. (188) *So Festus sent forces, both horsemen and footmen, to fall upon those that had been seduced by a certain impostor, who promised them deliverance and freedom from the miseries they were under,* if they would but follow him as far as the wilderness. Accordingly those forces that were sent destroyed both him that had deluded them, and those that were his followers also.[14]

The weapon was as big as the Persian *akinake* but was curved and like the Roman *sica*.[15] The curved sword (כידן) mentioned in Qumran scrolls[16] is too large for assassination-appropriate, stealthy, close assault. Further, Josephus describes the intrigue of the extremist political murderers, who were skilled, surreptitious infiltrators. Josephus in an account of the lawless bands which infested Judæa in these times, says (after relating how a notorious robber named Eleazar had been taken with his followers and sent in chains to Rome) [italics added]:[17]

3. (254) *When the country was purged of these, there sprang up another sort of robbers in Jerusalem, which were called Sicarii, who slew men in the daytime, and in the midst of the city; (255) this they did chiefly at the festivals, when they mingled themselves among the multitude, and concealed daggers under their garments, with which they stabbed those that were their enemies; and when any fell down dead, the murderers became a part of those that had indignation against them; by which means they appeared*

14. Flavius Josephus and William Whiston, *The Works of Josephus: Complete and Unabridged* (Peabody: Hendrickson, 1987), 537.

15. Flavius Josephus, *Bellum Judaicum* 2.254–255; Flavius Josephus, *Antiquitates Judaicae* 20.186.

16. *1QMilḥamah*, "The War Scroll" (*1QM*) 5:11–14.

17. J. Rawson Lumby, *The Acts of the Apostles*, Cambridge Greek Testament for Schools and Colleges (Cambridge: Cambridge University Press, 1891), 383.

persons of such reputation, that they could by no means be discovered. (256) The first man who was slain by them was Jonathan the high priest, after whose death many were slain every day, while the fear men were in of being so served, was more afflicting than the calamity itself; (257) and while everybody expected death every hour, as men do in war, so men were obliged to look before them, and to take notice of their enemies at a great distance; nor, if their friends were coming to them, durst they trust them any longer; but, in the midst of their suspicions and guarding of themselves, they were slain. Such was the celebrity of the plotters against them, and so cunning was their contrivance.[18]

This extremist, violent cabal of anti-Roman rebels[19] did "not shrink from political murder."[20] Such an assassin, a "cutthroat," "may kill secretly and treacherously any one he wishes to . . ."[21] William Whiston adds the denotation "insurgent," "a kind of rebel who constantly carried a dagger for killing enemies by surprise attack."[22] Louw and Nida portrayed the *modus operandi* of this anti-Roman faction:

18. Flavius Josephus and William Whiston, *The Works of Josephus: Complete and Unabridged* (Peabody: Hendrickson, 1987), 614; *B. J.* ii. 13. 3.

19. Flavius Josephus and William Whiston, *The Works of Josephus: Complete and Unabridged* (Peabody: Hendrickson, 1987), 614.

20. Horst Robert Balz and Gerhard Schneider, *Exegetical Dictionary of the New Testament* (Grand Rapids, Mich.: Eerdmans, 1990–), 243; (Josephus *Bellum Judaicum*, ii.254–57; Josephus, *Antiquities*, xx.186). Schürer, *History* I, 463; II, 602f.; D. M. Rhoads, *Israel in Revolution 6–74 C.E.* (1976) 111–22; O. Betz, *TDNT* VII, 278–82; *TWNT* X, 1264 (bibliography); K. Schubert, *Die jüdischen Religionsparteien in neutestamentlicher Zeit* (1970) 66–70; M. Hengel, *The Zealots* (1989), 46–53.

21. Joseph Henry Thayer, *A Greek-English Lexicon of the New Testament: Being Grimm's Wilke's Clavis Novi Testamenti* (New York: Harper & Brothers., 1889), 574–575: ". . . ἐκάλουν τοὺς λῃστὰς ἔχοντας ὑπὸ τοῖς κόλποις τὰ ξίφη [cf. 2, 13, 3]; also antt. 20, 8, 10 σικάριοι λῃσταί εἰσι χρώμενοι ξιφιδίοις παραπλησίοις μὲν τὸ μέγεθος τοῖς τῶν Περσῶν ἀκινάκαις, ἐπικαμπέσι δὲ καὶ ὁμοίοις ταῖς ὑπὸ Ῥωμαίων σίκαις καλουμέναις, ἀφ᾽ ὧν καὶ τὴν προσηγορίαν οἱ λῃστεύοντες ἔλαβον πολλοὺς ἀναιροῦντες.) [Syn. see φονεύς.]*"

22. Lexham Research Lexicon of the Greek New Testament, *Lexham Research Lexicons* (Bellingham, WA: Lexham Press, 2020).

Concealing under their garments that short sword of
theirs, and mingling with the multitude at the great
feasts, they stabbed in the crowd whom of their enemies
they would, and then, taking part with the bystanders
in exclamations of horror, effectually averted suspicion
from themselves.[23]

The term applied to the Egyptian false prophet described as follows who was matched by the Roman commander Festus:

5. (261) But there was an Egyptian false prophet that
did the Jews more mischief than the former; for he was
a cheat, and pretended to be a prophet also, and got together thirty thousand men that were deluded by him;
(262) these he led round about from the wilderness to
the mount which was called the Mount of Olives, and
was ready to break into Jerusalem by force from that
place; and if he could but once conquer the Roman garrison and the people, he intended to domineer over them
by the assistance of those guards of his that were to break
into the city with him, (263) but Felix prevented his attempt, and met him with his Roman soldiers, while all
the people assisted him in his attack upon them, inso-
much that, when it came to a battle, the Egyptian ran
away, with a few others, while the greatest part of those
that were with him were either destroyed or taken alive;
but the rest of the multitude were dispersed every one to
their own homes and there concealed themselves.[24]

Josephus also opines against a notorious robber named Eleazar, a
sicarii ringleader "among the lawless bands which infested Judæa
in these times," who had been taken with his followers and sent
enchained to be an open spectacle in Rome.[25] Otto Betz observes
the term *sicarii* came into force only during the years before the

23. Richard Chenevix Trench, *Synonyms of the New Testament* (London:
Macmillan and Co., 1880), 314.

24. Flavius Josephus and William Whiston, *The Works of Josephus: Complete
and Unabridged* (Peabody: Hendrickson, 1987), 614.

25. J. Rawson Lumby, *The Acts of the Apostles*, Cambridge Greek Testament
for Schools and Colleges (Cambridge: Cambridge University Press, 1891), 383;
Josephus, *Jewish War* 2.13.3.

outbreak of the rebellion crushed by Vespacian and Titus in A.D. 68 and it was directed against Jews friendly to the Romans rather than the Romans themselves. The designation clearly derived from the Romans.[26]

This Latin loan word[27] also appears in the "Letter to Didyme" (19.6 × 18.9 cm) within Oxyrhynchus Papyri, dating to the late second or early third century. The cursive letter regards the dispatch of various articles to his sister (possibly twin[28]), Didyme, with the term appearing in line 8. This letter reveals that the weapon was versatile, small enough to be used at table, and innocuous enough to be generally viewed as a table instrument:

1 . . . . Διδύμηι τῇ ἀδελφῇ

6 τοῦ ναυτικοῦ πανάριον ἐν ᾧ ὑάλαι λάγυνοι δ ὕγειαι

7 καὶ ἱμάντα δεδεμένον εἰς τὸ πανάριον καλὸν καὶ . . .

8 σικάρια· ἐξ αὐτῶν σεαυτῇ ἓν ἆρον. καὶ παρὰ Κάρπου

9 τοῦ δούλου Κλέωνος κόμισαι τὸ τοῦ παναρίου κλειδίον.

10 ἐὰν δέ σὺ μὴ δυνηθῇς ἀνοῖξαι τὸ πανάριον,

26. Josephus, *Bellum Judaicum*, V 7, p 280, as cited by Otto Betz, "Σικάριος," *Theological Dictionary of the New Testament* (Grand Rapids, MI: Eerdmans, 1964–), 281.

27. Lexham Research Lexicon of the Greek New Testament, *Lexham Research Lexicons* (Bellingham, WA: Lexham Press, 2020); Euripides: Eur., IT 390; Plutarchus: Plut., Praecepta 19; Josephus (Loeb): Ant 20.169; Ant 20.186; Wars 2.254; Wars 2.254–257; Wars 2.261; Oxyrhynchus Papyri: Oxyrhynchus Papyri 1294; Chance, J. Bradley. *Acts*. Edited by Leslie Andres and R. Alan Culpepper. Smyth & Helwys Bible Commentary. Macon, GA: Smyth & Helwys Publishing, Incorporated, 2007; Ac 21:38 from They Seized Paul, 21:27–40; Lumby, J. Rawson. *The Acts of the Apostles*. Cambridge Greek Testament for Schools and Colleges. Cambridge: Cambridge University Press, 1891; Acts 21:38 from 37–40. Paul Asks Leave to Address the Crowd.

28. Liddell, Scott, Jones (Unabridged) (Greek Entry): δίδῠμος [ῐ], η, ον, also ος, ον v.l. in Pi. P. 4.209, E. HF 656 (lyr.), Pl. Criti. 113e:—redupl. from δύο, double, twofold, Od. 19.227, etc.; δίδῠμαιν χειροῖν S. El. 206 (lyr.): also in sg., χερὶ διδύμαι with *both* hands, Pi. P. 2.9; δ. ἅλς, i. e. the Pontus and Bosporus, S. Ant. 967 (lyr.); δ. γένος AP 7.72 (Men.); δ. ξύλον forked, LXX Jo. 8.29; τὸ γλυκύ μοι δ., of a wife, IG 14.1974.

20 Διδύμη.[29]

Here, we learn that the dagger is small enough to be used for table usage, for the cutting of table bread (τὸ πανάριον, τοῦ παναρίου) that had to be opened from a bread basket with a key (κλειδίον). We learn from Josephus the swords were small enough to be maneuverable, as well as concealable—"They made use of small swords, not much different in length from the Persian acinacae, but somewhat crooked, and like the Roman sicae [or sickles] . . ."[30] An assassin's most effective tactic as an infiltrator may be anonymity, with a non-visible weapon, until it is wielded too late for the victim to react.

So significant was the terrorist-insurgent threat posed by the *sicarii* that Roman law was enacted specifically in response to the danger posed.[31] The law applied to the *sicarii*, as a legal *terminus technicus*, published under Sulla, in the *lex Cornelia*, with a specific, particular application to violent murderers, and their co-conspirators, who utilized this concealable, versatile, and maneuverable weapon.[32] The *lex Cornelia* applied to asymmetrical insurgency, including armed larcenous gangs (*latrones*) that banded together in organized crime, with rank and file in a command and control structure. The scope of the Roman law included guerrilla units, especially in rebellious provinces, but were not "considered worthy

29. Bernard P. Grenfell and Arthur S. Hunt, eds., "The Oxyrhynchus Papyri," *Egypt Exploration Fund: Graeco-Roman Branch* (London; Boston, MA; Edinburgh; New York; Linden, Berlin: The Offices of the Egypt Exploration Fund; Kegan Paul, Trench, Trübner & Co.; Bernard Quaritch; Asher & Co.; C. F. Clay; Humphrey Milford, 1914), 247–248; *cf.* Liddell, Scott, Jones (Unabridged) (Greek Entry): δίδυμος, *op. cit.*

30. Flavius Josephus and William Whiston, *The Works of Josephus: Complete and Unabridged* (Peabody: Hendrickson, 1987), 537.

31. Otto Betz, "Σικάριος," *Theological Dictionary of the New Testament* (Grand Rapids, MI: Eerdmans, 1964-) 278.

32. Quintillian, Institutio Oratoria 10, 1, 12: *Per abusionem sicarios etiam omnes vocamus, qui caedem telo quocumque commiserint.* Cf. T. Mommsen, *Röm. Strafrecht* (1899), 629.

of a Roman declaration of war."[33] Punishment of *sicarii* was torture and death via public crucifixion.[34]

Within the Greek New Testament, Otto Betz is keen in his observation that it "is quite understandable that Luke should use the term *sicarii*, especially on the lips of a Roman officer, for whom, as for the procurators, even unarmed participants in such freedom marches were *sicarii*." Further, whether the forty (40) who took an oath to neither eat nor drink until they had assassinated the Apostle Paul in Acts 23:12–15 is a "cookie-cutter" *modus operandi* in standard operation during the days of the *sicarri*—the "time, method and goal of the plot all support this" deduction. The assassination plot occurred under "under the procuratorship of Felix when the movement was at its height." The conspirators bonded and banded together via a common oath, against one they deemed to be an apostate, as well as "desecrator of the temple who had also been taken under protective custody" by the Roman Gentile occupying authorities.[35] As Arthur Headlam observed, the *sicarii* who "were so numerous at this time, illustrate the fanaticism, both religious and political, which culminated in the fall of Jerusalem."[36] They were responsible for the assassination of Jonathan, while high priest, the son of Annas, who also had been high priest (A.D. 55–56).[37] The successful strike to assassinate the son of the high

33. Pomponius According to Justinianus Digesta, 50, 16, 118 (ed. T. Mommsen [1870]): *Hostes hi sunt, qui nobis aut quibus nos publice bellum decrevimus; ceteri "latrones" aut "praedones" sunt.*

34. Paulus Sententiae, V, 23, 1 (ed. P. E. Huschke in Jurisprudentiae Anteiustinianae quae supersunt [1886], 551): *. . . humiliores vero aut in crucem tolluntur aut bestiis obiiciuntur,* as cited in Otto Betz, "Σικάριος," *Theological Dictionary of the New Testament* (Grand Rapids, MI: Eerdmans, 1964–), 278–279.

35. Otto Betz, "Σικάριος," *Theological Dictionary of the New Testament* (Grand Rapids, MI: Eerdmans, 1964–), 281.

36. Arthur Cayley Headlam, "Assassin," *A Dictionary of the Bible: Dealing with Its Language, Literature, and Contents Including the Biblical Theology* (New York; Edinburgh: Charles Scribner's Sons; T. & T. Clark, 1911–1912), 174.

37. Flavius Josephus, *Bellum Judaicum,* 2, 252, 256; According to *Antiquities,* 20, 185f. the *sicarii* flourished especially under Festus; according to Ant., 20, 204 Albinus extirpated many of them.

priest ushered in an era of politically motivated religious, as well as
religiously motivated political, chronic terrorism:

> After this, men lived in constant dread of them. They
> were conspicuous under Felix, who sent troops against
> them, and at a later date they took a leading part in the
> Jewish War, and in the disturbances which led to it, be-
> ing always amongst the most violent of the combatants.
> They held Masada, and from thence pillaged the country.
> Eventually some of them dispersed to Egypt and Cyrene,
> where, under the combined influence of want and fanati-
> cism, they introduced a reign of terror.[38]

Sicarii, as a political, sub-social, and guerrilla force, first consoli-
dated and deployed under the procuratorship of Felix. Not only as
thieves who lived off the land logistically, but militarily insurgents
who blended into the populace undercover, their first victim was
the current high-priest Jonathan,[39] as high-value a target as could
be eliminated within Jewry. Later when militant Jewish insurgents
split into separate factions under separate command and control
after the victory over Cestius, the Roman governor of Syria who
had marched toward Jerusalem but was turned back to retreat
north of Jerusalem at Gibeon. Josephus also applied the term *sicarii* for the followers of Menahem who after his assassination retreated into the fortress of Masada.[40] Josephus then uses the term
for the militant partisans who retreated, escaping to Egypt,[41] and
finally for the rebellious Jewish faction in Cyrene.[42]

38. Arthur Cayley Headlam, "Assassin," *A Dictionary of the Bible: Dealing with
Its Language, Literature, and Contents Including the Biblical Theology* (New York;
Edinburgh: Charles Scribner's Sons; T. & T. Clark, 1911–1912), 174.

39. Josephus, *Bellum Judaicum*, 2, 252, 256; According to *Antiquities*, 20, 185
f. the *sicarii* flourished especially under Festus; according to *Antiquities*, 20, 204
Albinus extirpated many of them.

40. Flavius Josephus, *The Jewish War* (*Bellum Judaicum*), Book 4, paras.
399–405, 516; also Book 2, paras. 253, 275, 297, 311 (William Whiston, transl.;
repr. Peabody, MA: Hendrickson, 1987).

41. *Op. cit.*, Book 7, paras. 409–419 (corresponding to Book 7, Whiston secs.
22–24) pace.biblico.it.

42. *Op. cit.*, Book 7, paras. 437–446.

The first-century political parties among the Jewish people in the land of Canaan included the Pharisees, Sadducees, Herodians, Hellenists, Essenes, and Zealots, of whom the Apostle Simon or Cephas (Matt. 10:4), later named by Christ "Peter," was considered a partisan. Both Pharisees and Sadducees sought to "go back" to pristine purity of Moses, although the former held to Mosaic law interpreted as per oral law, and latter held to Mosaic law alone. Ironically, the latter denied the resurrection (Matt. 22:23–33; Mark 12:18; Acts 23:8), but the former held to a literal resurrection (Acts 23:8). The Herodians sought to "go along" with the existing Roman-dominated Edomite usurping Herodian ruling clan (Luke 13:38). The Hellenists sought to "go with" the current prevailing Greek philosophies of the times. The Essenes sought to "go out," leaving the warp and woof of Jewish life in the hamlets, villages, and cities, residing in the caves of Qumran, in strictly disciplined religious communities, forebears of modern kibbutzes. The Zealots sought to "go against," seeking religious, political, and social independence from the yokes of Roman rule and multi-culture. The *Sicarri* would fall into the category of sub-faction within the "Zealots"—not all Zealots were *Sicarii*, but *Sicarii* would be considered armed, organized, militant, guerrilla Zealots, skilled at close assault assassination while blending into the population camouflaged.[43] According to Josephus, the Zealots began with Judas (the Galilean), son of Ezekias, who led a revolt in A.D. 6 because of a census done for tax purposes.[44] Led by Judas of Galilee, their religious zeal propelled the Jewish revolt against Rome in A.D. 6.[45] Prior to Judas of Galilee's rise to influence, no doubt the ascension of Herod the Great in 37 B.C. fomented the reaction of the religiously zealous against his Roman acquiescence. And even

43. Thomas Strong, "Zealot," *Holman Illustrated Bible Dictionary* (Nashville, TN: Holman Bible Publishers, 2003), 1700.

44. Charles W. Draper with Harrop Clayton, "Jewish Parties in the New Testament," *Holman Illustrated Bible Dictionary* (Nashville, TN: Holman Bible Publishers, 2003), 919.

45. Charles W. Draper with Harrop Clayton, "Jewish Parties in the New Testament," *Holman Illustrated Bible Dictionary* (Nashville, TN: Holman Bible Publishers, 2003), 919.

before Herod, the religious zeal of the Maccabean rebels continued into the Roman era.[46]

Luke in Acts 21:38 relates that the tribune of the Roman cohort stationed in the Antonia suspected that Paul was the Egyptian rebel who shortly before incited 4,000 *sicarii* to insurrection and then led them out into the desert. [47] Perhaps relatedly, Josephus tells of the enterprise of an Egyptian in two accounts which differ from one another in details. According to Josephus' *Bellum Judaicum*[48] this Egyptian claimed to be a prophet,[49] gathered together 30,000 men, and went via the desert to the Mount of Olives, from which point he sought to force his way into the city, overpower the Roman garrison, and set himself up as ruler.[50] Luke agrees with Josephus in simply speaking of "the Egyptian," in dating his venture under Felix[51] and in making a link with the wilderness. "It is quite understandable that Luke should use the term *sicarii*, especially on the lips of a Roman officer, for whom, as for the procurators, even unarmed participants in such freedom marches were *sicarii*."[52]

Otto Betz also qualifies the forty assassins who took an oath to neither drink nor eat until they had murdered Paul in Acts

46. Charles W. Draper with Harrop Clayton, "Jewish Parties in the New Testament," *Holman Illustrated Bible Dictionary* (Nashville, TN: Holman Bible Publishers, 2003), 919.

47. Otto Betz, "Σικάριος," *Theological Dictionary of the New Testament* (Grand Rapids, MI: Eerdmans, 1964–) 281.

48. Origen, *Contra Celsum*, in *Origenes Werke*, vol. 2 of *Die griechischen christlichen Schriftsteller der ersten drei Jahrhunderte*, ed. Paul Koetschau (Leipzig: J.C. Hinrichs, 1899), 261–263.

49. Flavius Josephus, *The Jewish War* (*Bellum Judaicum*), Book VI, paras. 826 ff., in *The Works of Josephus: Complete and Unabridged*, new updated edition (Peabody, MA: Hendrickson Publishers, 1987), translated by William Whiston. lexundria.com+15earlyjewishwritings.com+15en.wikipedia.org+15.

50. Otto Betz, "Σικάριος," *Theological Dictionary of the New Testament* (Grand Rapids, MI: Eerdmans, 1964–), 281.

51. Otto Betz, "Σικάριος," *Theological Dictionary of the New Testament* (Grand Rapids, MI: Eerdmans, 1964–).

52. Otto Betz, "Σικάριος," *Theological Dictionary of the New Testament* (Grand Rapids, MI: Eerdmans, 1964–)

23:12–15 is not standard *sicarii* modus operandi—"time, method and goal of the plot" are distinguishable. Their motive, objective, and stratagem was to rid Jewry of an apostate who they believed defiled their most holy site: "Their objective was to remove a false teacher and desecrator of the temple who had also been taken under protective custody by the Gentiles."[53] Josephus, paid and puppeted by the Roman occupiers, adopts the standpoint of Roman law when he calls the hated freedom fighters of the first Jewish revolt "robbers"[54] and "assassins" (σικαρίους).[55] What distinguished them was not doctrine—they shared this with Judas, the founder of the Zealot party[56]—but the courageous nature of their effort, which held life cheap, whether their own or that of others (τολμᾶν, Ant, 20, 165).[57] The weapon of assassination was used especially when Felix took steps of ruthless severity against the bands in open country.[58]

Otto Benz explores the psychology of the Jewish *sicarii*, pinpointing their core motivations.

53. Otto Betz, "Σικάριος," *Theological Dictionary of the New Testament* (Grand Rapids, MI: Eerdmans, 1964–) 281.

54. Origen, *Contra Celsum*, in *Origenes Werke*, vol. 2 of *Die griechischen christlichen Schriftsteller der ersten drei Jahrhunderte*, ed. Paul Koetschau (Leipzig: J.C. Hinrichs, 1899), 884, lines 32ff.

55. *Die griechischen christlichen Schriftsteller der ersten drei Jahrhunderte* (Leipzig: J.C. Hinrichs) IV, 258, 18ff.

56. *Cf. Bellum Judaicum*, 2. 118 with 7, 418 f. In *Bellum Judaicum*, 7, 254 Jos. associates the *sicarii* chronologically with Judas. Since their leaders Menahem and Eleazar b. Ari were relatives of this Judas (Bell., 2, 433; 7, 253) their link with him was also dynastic and organisational, Hengel, 50. Finally Judas, like his son Menahem (Bell., 2, 433 f.), forced his followers to carry weapons. Josephus, *Jewish War* 2.56; Josephus, *Antiquities* 17.251ff.

57. Josephus, *Bellum Judaicum* 2, 254–260 contrasts with the *sicarii* the fanatics and deceivers whose "hands were purer"; these popular charismatic leaders feared the use of violence and counted on a divine miracle which would announce symbolically the dawn of the age of salvation. Otto Betz, "Σικάριος," *Theological Dictionary of the New Testament* (Grand Rapids, MI: Eerdmans, 1964–).

58. Josephus, *Bellum Judaicum* 2, 253.

The reasons which drove the *sicarii* to act were not blind nationalism nor an excessive lust for domination. The *sicarii* were motivated, not by ungodliness, unrighteousness or fanaticism (Bell, 7, 260 and 437), but by passionate zeal and active self-sacrifice for God's honour and the Torah. The maxim that God alone is to be honoured as Lord was consistently applied. Josephus is clear that they accepted suicide or martyrdom rather than the yoke of Roman rule, Bell, 7, 386–401, 410, 418 f. According to their view the majesty of God was infringed not merely by the Romans, who wanted the emperor to be recognised as ruler (7, 418 f.) and who desecrated the land by taxes, coins, statues and the census, but also by Jews friendly to the Romans, who as renegades were regarded as the equivalent of Gentiles (7, 255).

Although not theologically driven, the *sicarii* viewed the compromising priests as not sacrosanct and as guilty as the Jews who served the Romans as ruthless, heartless tax collectors:

Indeed, for the *sicarii* the priests who engaged in a politics of compromise were seducing the people into idolatry, and what Jos. ascribed to a propensity to cruelty (7, 256) really derived from obedience to God's Law, which commanded that apostates and even whole districts which were idolatrous should be rooted out by fire and sword, Deut. 13:7–19. By purgative action of this kind they sought to prepare the way for God's coming and to prevent the land from being smitten with a ban through God's wrath, cf. Mal. 4:6. Stealing and confiscating the goods of the rich (Bell, 4, 402–405, 516; 7, 254; Ant, 20, 185–187), destruction of palaces and burning of archives with promissory notes (Bell, 2, 426–432), cannot be set to the account of greed (7, 256) but were meant to serve the overthrow of the unrighteous mammon and the establishment of the eternal jubilee of freedom and equality.[59]

---

59. Otto Betz, "Σικάριος," *Theological Dictionary of the New Testament* (Grand Rapids, MI: Eerdmans, 1964–), 279–280.

In some Rabbinic writings the name *sicarii* (סִיקָרִימ/ין) at times is applied to Zealots (קַנָּאִים), although with no mention of assassination plots or intent. Zealots who supported the first revolt are called *sicarii* not because of any assassination modus operandi but because of their express attitude to support violence in rebellion. Otto Betz describes variegated terrorist acts in support of armed rebellion:

> According to Makkot [Talmudic tractate "Makkot" (Hebrew: מַכּוֹת), which means "lashes" or "beatings" in the Order of Nezikin (Damages) in the Mishnah and Talmud], 1, 6 the population of Jerusalem kept fig-cakes concealed in water because of the *sicarii*. According to *Eka rabbati*, on 4:4 the *sicarii* destroyed the conduit which supplied Jerusalem from Etam.[60] According to Ab RNat [Avot de-Rabbi Natan (Hebrewאבות דרבי נתן), an extracanonical rabbinic work often considered a tosefta or expanded commentary on *Pirkei Avot* ("Ethics of the Fathers")], they burned the grain stocks which a rich man of Jerusalem had stored up in the event of siege. Josephus confirms these violent acts: confiscation and destruction of stocks occurred esp. in struggles between the various rebel groups, Bell, 5, 21–26; cf. Tac. Hist., V, 12. According to Qohr (Qohelet or Ecclesiastes) on 7:12 the head of the *sicarii* (רֹאשׁ סְקָרִים), Ben Battiach, the son-in-law of Rabbi Jochanan b. Zakkai, was responsible for the burning of the grain. This Zealot, identified by some as Simon bar Giora, is called the "'daddy' of assassins" (אַבָּא סִיקָרָא) in the parb. Git [Parashat Gitin of the Babylonian Talmud] 56a. A *sicaricon law* (סִיקָרִקוֹן) is also mentioned in the Rabb in *Bikkurim*, 1, 2; Gittin, 6, 5; S. Dt 297 on 26:2 etc. It relates to property, especially landed property, which during and after the first revolt had been expropriated by the Romans. This law has reference

---

60. Otto Betz remarks, "With S. Buber, 1899) מדרש איכה רבה) one should read מְסִיקָרִים and מַעֲיטָם here. Possible this was terrorism against the conduit Pilate had built with temple funds, cf. *Bellum.*, 2, 175; Hengel, 51; Abot of Rabbi Nathan—an extracanonical Rabbinic tractate (Strack, *Einl.*, 72)," as cited in Otto Betz, "Σικάριος," *Theological Dictionary of the New Testament* (Grand Rapids, MI: Eerdmans, 1964–).

to the Jewish *sicarii* only to the degree that the property confiscated was mostly that of zealous patriots who had fled to the desert.[61]

Some references to the *sicarii* appear in the Church Fathers. Hippolytus, for instance, mentions the *sicarii* in an account of the Essenes which he took from Josephus, where he equates them with the Zealots but erroneously thinks they were a class of Essenes.[62] They are characterized by the dogma of God's sole sovereignty, which they maintained[63] even to death, and by sharp hostility to images. Men who speak of God and His laws but will not accept circumcision are mentioned as the victims of assassination.[64] Origen refers to the *sicarii* in a different connection, as Samaritans, not accurately.[65] Yet, dubious accounts of the *sicarii* notwithstand-

61. Abot of Rabbi Nathan (Ab RNat)—an extracanonical Rabbinic tractate (Hermann L. Strack, *Einleitung in den Talmud* (Introduction to the Talmud), §72—; Otto Betz, "Σικάριος," *Theological Dictionary of the New Testament* (TDNT) (Grand Rapids, MI: Eerdmans, 1964-), 280, comparing the Exc.: "Das Sikarikongesetz" in Martin Hengel, *The Zealots: Investigations into the Jewish Freedom Movement in the Period from Herod I until 70 A.D.*, trans. David Smith (Edinburgh: T&T Clark, 1989), originally published in German (Leipzig, 1961); Jastrow, *sub verbo* "Sicarius" סִיקָרִיקוֹן thinks the word is a corruption of χαισαρίχιον, "Caesar's tax" or imperial designation. Marcus Jastrow, *Dictionary of the Targumim, the Talmud Babli and Yerushalmi, and the Midrashic Literature.*

62. Hippolytus of Rome, *Refutation of All Heresies* (Ref.), IX, 26, 2, cf. Josephus, *Bellum Jadaicum*, (The Jewish War), Book 2, §§119–161. In reality the features here ascribed to the different groups are probably all characteristic of the Zealots, Hengel, 74 ff., as cited by Otto Betts, *op. cit., "in the work previously cited"* in TDNT.

63. Martin Hengel, "Ζηλωτής," in *Theological Dictionary of the New Testament*, vol. 7, ed. Gerhard Friedrich, trans. Geoffrey W. Bromiley (Grand Rapids, MI: Eerdmans, 1971), 282.

64. Psalm 50:16 was probably given as a reason: "To the wicked God saith: Why dost thou proclaim my statutes and take my covenant in thy mouth?" Origen, of Alexandria (A.D. 185–254), pupil of Clement of Alexandria, and most learned and fruitful representative of ancient Christian scholarship and culture, ed. by different scholars in *Die griech, christl. Schriftsteller der ersten 3 Jahrhunderte* (Berlin, Akademie Verlag), 1899 ff.

65. Origen of Alexandria (c. 185–254), *Contra Celsum*, Book II, Chapter 13, II, 13 (*Die griechischen christlichen Schriftsteller der ersten drei Jahrhunderte* (GCS = Greek Christian Writers of the First Three Centuries, 2, 142, lines 10–22). He

ing, they left their mark of violent infiltration, calculated terrorism, and committed lethality—whether against their oppressors or their own people who collaborate with them.

Parallels Between the Wound and Scripture—A Biblical Analogical Analysis

Some have drawn conclusions regarding the particular wound inflicted upon the former President by the assassin in his failed assassination attempt. The right ear of the former President was pierced, most evidently, during the attack on July 13, 2024. Biblical prophecy, however, is marked by specificity, particularity, and actuality, in order to prove beyond doubt that the prophetic prediction is divine in provenance. God proves his prophetic Word by fulfilling his prophetic Word—objectively, definitely, and without ambiguity. Consider Peter's words, "We also have a more sure word of prophecy" (2 Pet. 1:19).[66]

The following is a list of each occurrence, from both the Hebrew Bible, and Greek New Testament, of passages accurately translated into English "right ear":

> Exod. 29:20 Then shalt thou kill the ram, and take of his blood, and put *it* upon the tip of the right ear of Aaron, and upon the tip of the right ear of his sons, and upon

---

says the Samaritans were thought to be *sicarii* because they clung fast to circumcision. Hadrian compared this to castration, which had been forbidden since Domitian and placed under the penalties of the *lex Cornelia*. (The *lex Cornelia*, enacted in 81 B.C., addressed extortion, especially by provincial governors, abandonment of posts by governors, and general crimes including battery.)

66. 2 Pet 1:19: "We have also a more sure word of prophecy; whereunto ye do well that ye take heed, as unto a light that shineth in a dark place, until the day dawn, and the day star arise in your hearts:καὶ ἔχομεν βεβαιότερον τὸν προφητικὸν λόγον, ᾧ καλῶς ποιεῖτε προσέχοντες ὡς λύχνῳ φαίνοντι ἐν αὐχμηρῷ τόπῳ, ἕως οὗ ἡμέρα διαυγάσῃ καὶ φωσφόρος ἀνατείλῃ ἐν ταῖς καρδίαις ὑμῶν." *The Holy Bible: King James Version*, Electronic Edition of the 1900 Authorized Version. (Bellingham, WA: Logos Research Systems, Inc., 2009), occurrence of "more sure word of prophecy" with Greek New Testament LGNTI: SBL parallels.

the thumb of their right hand, and upon the great toe of their right foot, and sprinkle the blood upon the altar round about.וְשָׁחַטְתָּ אֶת־הָאַיִל וְלָקַחְתָּ מִדָּמוֹ וְנָתַתָּה עַל־תְּנוּךְ

אֹזֶן אַהֲרֹן וְעַל־תְּנוּךְ אֹזֶן בָּנָיו הַיְמָנִית וְעַל־בֹּהֶן יָדָם הַיְמָנִית וְעַל־

בֹּהֶן רַגְלָם הַיְמָנִית וְזָרַקְתָּ אֶת־הַדָּם עַל־הַמִּזְבֵּחַ סָבִיב:

Lev. 8:23 And he slew *it*; and Moses took of the blood of it, and put *it* upon the tip of Aaron's <u>right ear</u>, and upon the thumb of his right hand, and upon the great toe of his right foot.וַיִּשְׁחָט | וַיִּקַּח מֹשֶׁה מִדָּמוֹ וַיִּתֵּן עַל־תְּנוּךְ אֹזֶן־אַהֲרֹן

הַיְמָנִית וְעַל־בֹּהֶן יָדוֹ הַיְמָנִית וְעַל־בֹּהֶן רַגְלוֹ הַיְמָנִית:

Lev. 8:24 And he brought Aaron's sons, and Moses put of the blood upon the tip of their <u>right ear</u>, and upon the thumbs of their right hands, and upon the great toes of their right feet: and Moses sprinkled the blood upon the altar round about.וַיַּקְרֵב אֶת־בְּנֵי אַהֲרֹן וַיִּתֵּן מֹשֶׁה מִן־הַדָּם עַל־

תְּנוּךְ אָזְנָם הַיְמָנִית וְעַל־בֹּהֶן יָדָם הַיְמָנִית וְעַל־בֹּהֶן רַגְלָם הַיְמָנִית

וַיִּזְרֹק מֹשֶׁה אֶת־הַדָּם עַל־הַמִּזְבֵּחַ סָבִיב:

Lev. 14:14 And the priest shall take *some* of the blood of the trespass offering, and the priest shall put *it* upon the tip of the <u>right ear</u> of him that is to be cleansed, and upon the thumb of his right hand, and upon the great toe of his right foot:וְלָקַח הַכֹּהֵן מִדַּם הָאָשָׁם וְנָתַן הַכֹּהֵן עַל־תְּנוּךְ

אֹזֶן הַמִּטַּהֵר הַיְמָנִית וְעַל־בֹּהֶן יָדוֹ הַיְמָנִית וְעַל־בֹּהֶן רַגְלוֹ הַיְמָנִית:

Lev. 14:17 And of the rest of the oil that *is* in his hand shall the priest put upon the tip of the <u>right ear</u> of him that is to be cleansed, and upon the thumb of his right hand, and upon the great toe of his right foot, upon the blood of the trespass offering:וּמִיֶּתֶר הַשֶּׁמֶן אֲשֶׁר עַל־כַּפּוֹ יִתֵּן

הַכֹּהֵן עַל־תְּנוּךְ אֹזֶן הַמִּטַּהֵר הַיְמָנִית וְעַל־בֹּהֶן יָדוֹ הַיְמָנִית וְעַל־בֹּהֶן

רַגְלוֹ הַיְמָנִית עַל דַּם הָאָשָׁם:

Lev. 14:25 And he shall kill the lamb of the trespass offering, and the priest shall take *some* of the blood of the trespass offering, and put *it* upon the tip of the <u>right ear</u> of him that is to be cleansed, and upon the thumb of his right hand, and upon the great toe of his right foot:וְשָׁחַט אֶת־כֶּבֶשׂ הָאָשָׁם וְלָקַח הַכֹּהֵן מִדַּם הָאָשָׁם וְנָתַן עַל־תְּנוּךְ

אֹזֶן־הַמִּטַּהֵר הַיְמָנִית וְעַל־בֹּהֶן יָדוֹ הַיְמָנִית וְעַל־בֹּהֶן רַגְלוֹ הַיְמָנִית:

<u>Lev. 14:28</u> And the priest shall put of the oil that *is* in his hand upon the tip of the <u>right ear</u> of him that is to be cleansed, and upon the thumb of his right hand, and upon the great toe of his right foot, upon the place of the blood of the trespass offering:‏וְנָתַן הַכֹּהֵן מִן־הַשֶּׁמֶן | אֲשֶׁר עַל־ כַּפּוֹ עַל־תְּנוּךְ אֹזֶן הַמִּטַּהֵר הַיְמָנִית וְעַל־בֹּהֶן יָדוֹ הַיְמָנִית וְעַל־בֹּהֶן רַגְלוֹ הַיְמָנִית עַל־מְקוֹם דַּם הָאָשָׁם:

<u>Luke 22:50</u> And one of them smote the servant of the high priest, and cut off his <u>right ear</u>. καὶ ἐπάταξεν εἷς τις ἐξ αὐτῶν τοῦ ἀρχιερέως τὸν δοῦλον καὶ ἀφεῖλεν τὸ_οὖς αὐτοῦ τὸ_δεξιόν.

<u>John 18:10</u> Then Simon Peter having a sword drew it, and smote the high priest's servant, and cut off his <u>right ear</u>. The servant's name was Malchus. Σίμων οὖν Πέτρος ἔχων μάχαιραν εἵλκυσεν αὐτὴν καὶ ἔπαισεν τὸν τοῦ ἀρχιερέως δοῦλον καὶ ἀπέκοψεν αὐτοῦ τὸ ὠτάριον τὸ_δεξιόν. ἦν δὲ ὄνομα τῷ δούλῳ Μάλχος.[67]

While certain biblical passages may appear to parallel the events of July 13, 2024, they cannot be considered prophetic of this specific incident, as they do not contain the precise details regarding the person, place, timing, and nature of the attempted assassination. Biblical prophecy is specific and particular in content, to create an objective, definite, and undeniable fulfillment. Although the right ear signifies various spiritual lessons—the power of Jesus to heal and the consecration of priests—the content of the passages above is not prophetic but historical. A parallel between a current event and a biblical historical event is not necessarily a fulfilled prophecy, because a fulfilled prophecy requires a definite prediction. The Greek term translated as prophecy means either forthtelling the truth, or foretelling the future. References to the "right ear" are in specific semantic contexts in Scripture and a future occurrence.

The Greek (προφητεία) and Hebrew (נְבוּאָה: נָבִיא) terms for "prophecy" in the original Testaments mean foretelling a future

---

67. *The Holy Bible: King James Version*, Electronic Edition of the 1900 Authorized Version. (Bellingham, WA: Logos Research Systems, Inc., 2009), occurrences of "right ear" with Hebrew Masoretic original (7X) and Greek New Testament SBL Edition original (2X).

event or forthtelling a preachment. Bauer, Danker, Arndt and Gingrich's lexicon describes the Greek term προφητεία as follows:

προφητεία, ας, ἡ (προφήτης; Lucian, Alex. 40; 60; Heliod. 1, 22, 7; 1, 33, 2; 2, 27, 1; Ps.-Callisth. 2, 1, 3 [prophetic office]; CIG 2880, 4–6; 2881, 4; 5; OGI 494, 8f; PTebt 294, 8; 295, 10; LXX, Test12Patr; AscIs 3:21 and 31; Philo, Joseph., Just.; Ath. 9, 2)

1. act of interpreting divine will or purpose, *prophetic activity* αἱ ἡμέραι τῆς προφητείας αὐτῶν Rv 11:6. μισθοὺς λαμβάνει τῆς προφητείας αὐτοῦ *he accepts pay for his activity as prophet* Hm 11:12.

2. the gift of interpreting divine will or purpose, *gift of prophesying* (Iren. 1, 13, 4 [Harv. I 120, 4]), of Rahab 1 Cl 12:8. Of Christians Ro 12:6; 1 Cor 12:10; 13:2, 8 v.l.; 14:22. The pl. of various kinds and grades of prophetic gifts 13:8; 1 Th 5:20 (here mng. 3b is also prob.). τὸ πνεῦμα τῆς πρ. *the spirit of prophecy* Rv 19:10.

3. the utterance of one who interprets divine will or purpose, *prophecy* (Jos., Ant. 9, 119; Just., D. 30, 2; 54, 2 al. Of the Sibyl: Theoph. Ant. 2, 36 [p. 190, 10]).

a. of OT inspired statement (Orig., C. Cels. 1, 51, 23; Hippol., Ref. 6, 19, 7; Theoph. Ant. 3, 25 [p. 256, 20]) ἡ προφητεία Ἡσαΐου Mt 13:14 (Just.. D. 50, 2 al.). αἱ προφητεῖαι beside ὁ νόμος Μωσέως (Μωϋσέως is better; s. Bihlmeyer p. xxxvi) ISm 5:1. Gener. of OT sayings 2 Pt 1:20f (but P72 appears to distinguish prophecy and OT writing: προφητεία καὶ γραφή); B 13:4 (Gen. 48:11; Just., A I, 54, 7 Μωϋσέως).

b. of inspired statements by Christian prophets ἐν προφητείαι *in the form of a prophetic saying* 1 Cor 14:6; 1 Th 5:20 (s. 2 above); 1 Ti 1:18; 4:14. οἱ λόγοι τῆς πρ. *the words of the prophecy* Rv 1:3. οἱ λόγοι τῆς πρ. τοῦ βιβλίου τούτου *the words of prophecy in this book* 22:7, 10, 18. οἱ λόγ. τοῦ βιβλίου τῆς πρ. ταύτης *the words of this book of prophecy* vs. 19.—DELG s.v. φημί II A. M-M. TW.[68]

68. Walter Bauer, Frederick W. Danker, William F. Arndt, and F. W. Gingrich, *A GreekEnglish Lexicon of the New Testament and Other Early Christian Literature*, 3rd ed. (Chicago: University of Chicago Press, 2000), s.v. "entryword,"

The Hebrew term for "prophecy" is נָבִיא :נְבוּאָה, meaning a "prophetic utterance" (*cf.* Neh. 6:12; 2 Chron. 15.8; recorded in writing 2 Chron. 9:2), is similar to the Greek term.[69]

Current events are acts of divine providence. If God is sovereign (Psalm 103:19; 104:24; Matt. 10:29–31), all things that happen are by His decree (Isa. 28:9). As the Puritan John Flavel remarked: "Providence has a voice, if we have an ear." Whatever happens is under divine sovereign control. The Westminster Shorter Catechism remarks:

> Q. 11. *What are God's works of providence? A.* God's works of providence are, his most holy, wise, and powerful preserving and governing all his creatures, and all their actions.[70]

The Westminster Larger Catechism amplifies the above doctrine of divine providence as per Romans 11:36, by adding to the definition above of the Short Catechism "to his own glory."[71] The Westminster Confession of Faith further amplifies the doctrine of divine providence:

para. 1.

69. "נְבוּאָה נָבִיא" Ludwig Koehler and Walter Baumgartner, *The Hebrew and Aramaic Lexicon of the Old Testament* (HALOT), 3rd alphabetical ed., 2 vols. (Leiden: Brill, 2001), 2: 660.

70. Westminster Assembly, *The Westminster Confession of Faith: Edinburgh Edition* (Philadelphia: William S. Young, 1851), 390.

Psalm 145:17. The Lord is righteous in all his ways, and holy in all his works.

Psalm 104:24. O Lord, how manifold are thy works! in wisdom hast thou made them all: the earth is full of thy riches. Isa. 28:29. This also cometh forth from the Lord of hosts, which is wonderful in counsel, and excellent in working.

Heb. 1:3. Who being the brightness of his glory, and the express image of his person, and upholding all things by the word of his power, when he had by himself purged our sins, sat down on the right hand of the Majesty on high.

Psalm 103:19. The Lord hath prepared his throne in the heavens; and his kingdom ruleth over all. Matt. 10:29. Are not two sparrows sold for a farthing? and one of them shall not fall on the ground without your Father. Ver. 30. But the very hairs of your head are all numbered. Ver. 31. Fear ye not therefore; ye are of more value than many sparrows.

71. *Cf.* Isa. 63.14: "As a beast goeth down into the valley, the Spirit of the Lord caused him to rest; so didst thou lead thy people, to make thyself a glorious name."

God, the great Creator of all things, doth uphold, direct, dispose, and govern all creatures, actions, and things, from the greatest even to the least, by his most wise and holy providence, according to his infallible foreknowledge, and the free and immutable counsel of his own will, to the praise of the glory of his wisdom, power, justice, goodness, and mercy.

Providentially, the life of a former President was preserved, and, as per numerous passages of Scripture (Heb. 1:3; Dan. 4:34, 35; Matt.10:29, 30; Psalm 145:7; Acts 15:18; Psalm 33:10–11; Isa. 63:14; Gen. 45:7; Psalm 145:7), the act is a message to any and all who have ears to hear (Rev. 2:7, 17).

Thou Shalt Not Kill[72]—The Sixth (6th) Commandment Remains as Universal Law, and No One Is Above It

The biblical theology against homicide in general is distilled in one thesis—the taking of human life by malice aforethought is a definite capital offense. The biblical theology that prohibits the unlawful taking of human life consists of and revolves around several core passages. The first institution of justice for murder appears in the context of the Noahic covenant:

Genesis 9:4–6:

4 But flesh with the life thereof, *which is* the blood thereof, shall ye not eat. 5 And surely your blood of your lives will I require; at the hand of every beast will I require it, and at the hand of man; at the hand of every man's brother will I require the life of man. 6 Whoso sheddeth man's blood, by man shall his blood be shed: for in the image of God made he man. [73]

72. *The Holy Bible: King James Version*, Electronic Edition of the 1900 Authorized Version. (Bellingham, WA: Logos Research Systems, Inc., 2009), Exodus 20.13.

73. *The Holy Bible: King James Version*, Electronic Edition of the 1900 Authorized Version. (Bellingham, WA: Logos Research Systems, Inc., 2009), Ge 9:4–Dt 19:13.

In the Noahic Covenant, the moral law against murder, with the necessary sanction of capital punishment, instituted a foundation for social order. As Allen P. Ross expounds on Genesis 9:6:

> With Noah's new beginning came a covenant. It was necessary now to have a covenant with obligations for mankind and a promise from God. Because of the Flood's destruction of life people might begin to think that God holds life cheap and assume that taking life is a small matter. This covenant shows that life is sacred and that man is not to destroy man, who is made in the image of God.
>
> In essence, then, this covenant was established to ensure the stability of nature. It helped guarantee the order of the world. People would also learn that human law was necessary for the stability of life and that wickedness should not go unchecked as it had before.[74]

Capital punishment, life for life, is a core principle in social order.

Predating the Genesis 9 account of the institution of the Noahic covenant, with its *lex talionis* for murder (Gen. 9:6), is the case of the first murder, Cain's murder of his younger, more conscientious brother, Abel (Genesis 4). Some have opined that in this case, God suspended His own universal law. The phenomenon of God suspending His own law is found in other cases in the Hebrew Bible—the command of casting out (with possible death) Hagar and her child Ishmael (Genesis 16 and 21), the command to Abram to sacrifice Isaac (Gen. 22:1–19; *cf.* vs. 2), the command to Isaiah to be unclad (Isa. 20:1–6), and the command of Hosea to marry the prostitute Gomer (Hosea 1). As Paul interprets particularly Genesis 21, "which things are an allegory ($\alpha\lambda\lambda\epsilon\gamma\rho\iota\alpha$)" (Gal. 4:21–31, interpreting Gen. 21:8–21), the case is a preachment of "the two covenants." By analogy, the sacrifice of the Son of God by the Father is emblemized in Genesis 22. Christ's humiliation

---

74. Allen P. Ross, "Genesis," in *The Bible Knowledge Commentary: An Exposition of the Scriptures*, ed. J. F. Walvoord and R. B. Zuck (Wheaton, IL: Victor Books, 1985), 40.

is emblemized by Isaiah's humiliation (Isa. 20:1–6; *cf.* vs. 2). And, God married an unfaithful Israel ((Jer. 2:23–37; 3:1–5).

The general *lex taliones* is explicit in Exodus 21:12–14, 24–25, establishing the judicial ideal of balancing the crime with the punishment. A punishment must fit the crime. Punishment must be fair, just and equitable—the governed must consent, in general, that the adjudications of the governors are fair. "Eye for eye, tooth for tooth, life for life," the *lex taliones*, applies as the bulwark of social justice. Note in the case of a stillborn child caused by physical altercation in Exodus 21, the death is to be treated as "life for life":

> Exodus 21:22 If men strive, and hurt a woman with child, so that her fruit depart *from her*, and yet no mischief follow: he shall be surely punished, according as the woman's husband will lay upon him; and he shall pay as the judges *determine*. 23 And if *any* mischief follow, then thou shalt give life for life . . .

The life of the preborn child, valued as created in God's image, is to be adjudicated as per Genesis 9:6, "whoso sheddeth man's blood, by him shall his blood be shed."

The *lex taliones* appears in the following texts, as a general equity, but also the particular justice of capital punishment for murder;

> Exodus 21:24 Eye for eye, tooth for tooth, hand for hand, foot for foot,

> Exodus 21:25 Burning for burning, wound for wound, stripe for stripe. [75]

> Leviticus 24:19 And if a man cause a blemish in his neighbour; as he hath done, so shall it be done to him;

> Leviticus 24:20 Breach for breach, eye for eye, tooth for tooth: as he hath caused a blemish in a man, so shall it be done to him *again*.

---

75. *The King James Version*, electronic ed. (Accordance Bible Software, OakTree Software, Inc., version 14, 2025), accessed July 21, 2025.

> Leviticus 24:21 And he that killeth a beast, he shall restore it: and he that killeth a man, he shall be put to death. [76]

> Deuteronomy 19:20 And those which remain shall hear, and fear, and shall henceforth commit no more any such evil among you.

> Deuteronomy 19:21 And thine eye shall not pity; *but* life *shall go* for life, eye for eye, tooth for tooth, hand for hand, foot for foot.[77]

The laws of Moses divide into apodictic and casuistic categories—apodictic laws are general with open application in scope; casuistic laws apply to specific cases with application to analogous fact patterns. The following is apodictic law, applying universally in scope:

> Exodus 20:13:

> 13 Thou shalt not kill.[78]

The following is apodictic law, with an added specific casuistic focus:

> Exodus 21:12–14:

> 12 He that smiteth a man, so that he die, shall be surely put to death. 13 And if a man lie not in wait, but God deliver *him* into his hand; then I will appoint thee a place whither he shall flee. 14 But if a man come presumptuously upon his neighbour, to slay him with guile; thou shalt take him from mine altar, that he may die.[79]

76. *The King James Version*, electronic ed. (Accordance Bible Software, OakTree Software, Inc., version 14, 2025), accessed July 21, 2025.

77. *The King James Version*, electronic ed. (Accordance Bible Software, OakTree Software, Inc., version 14, 2025), accessed July 21, 2025.

78. *The Holy Bible: King James Version*, Electronic Edition of the 1900 Authorized Version. (Bellingham, WA: Logos Research Systems, Inc., 2009), Ge 9:4–Dt 19:13.

79. *The Holy Bible: King James Version*, Electronic Edition of the 1900 Authorized Version. (Bellingham, WA: Logos Research Systems, Inc., 2009), Ge 9:4–Dt 19:13.

Capital punishment is instituted categorically for murder in Exodus 21:12. However, in the case of no malice aforethought, the
perpetrator could flee for refuge to be heard by judges in a more
distant setting, to forestall familial revenge. If presumptuous guile
leads to murder, capital punishment is to require the life of the
criminal perpetrator. Leviticus echoes the same apodictic law, that
there must be "life for life":

> Leviticus 24:17 And he that killeth any man shall surely
> be put to death.

> Leviticus 24:21 And he that killeth a beast, he shall re-
> store it: and he that killeth a man, he shall be put to death.

"Life for life" is the law of the Hebrew Bible.

In Rabbinic tradition (Talmud Bavli, *Bava Kamma* 83b–84a)
the *lex talionis* is interpreted conceptually and quantitively, not
literally and qualitatively. For instance, the loss of an eye would
not result in the juridical punishment of gouging out the eye of the
perpetrator. Rather, the monetary value of the eye would be posited by the judges, and a just fine would be applied to the perpetrator. Rather than physically removing an offender's eye, monetary
compensation was assessed for the damage caused in the loss. Factors weighed in the equation of justice would include the value of
the eye, pain, suffering, medical costs, as compensatory, and even
additional payment for punitive punishment.[80]

Unlike the Code of Hammurabi, in murder cases there can be
no mere fine as punishment, because of the value of God-created
human life. Life for life requires capital punishment (Gen. 9:6). As
Number 35:31 requires, there can be no כפר, meaning atonement,
satisfaction, fine, or restitution by compensation.

> Numbers 35:12–33:

> 12 And they shall be unto you cities for refuge from the
> avenger; that the manslayer die not, until he stand before
> the congregation in judgment. 13 And of these cities
> which ye shall give six cities shall ye have for refuge. 14

---

80. *Babylonian Talmud (Bavli), Bava Kamma* 83b–84a.

Ye shall give three cities on this side Jordan, and three cities shall ye give in the land of Canaan, *which* shall be cities of refuge. 15 These six cities shall be a refuge, *both* for the children of Israel, and for the stranger, and for the sojourner among them: that every one that killeth any person unawares may flee thither. 16 And if he smite him with an instrument of iron, so that he die, he *is* a murderer: the murderer shall surely be put to death. 17 And if he smite him with throwing a stone, wherewith he may die, and he die, he *is* a murderer: the murderer shall surely be put to death. 18 Or *if* he smite him with an hand weapon of wood, wherewith he may die, and he die, he *is* a murderer: the murderer shall surely be put to death. 19 The revenger of blood himself shall slay the murderer: when he meeteth him, he shall slay him. 20 But if he thrust him of hatred, or hurl at him by laying of wait, that he die; 21 Or in enmity smite him with his hand, that he die: he that smote *him* shall surely be put to death; *for* he *is* a murderer: the revenger of blood shall slay the murderer, when he meeteth him. 22 But if he thrust him suddenly without enmity, or have cast upon him any thing without laying of wait, 23 Or with any stone, wherewith a man may die, seeing *him* not, and cast *it* upon him, that he die, and *was* not his enemy, neither sought his harm: 24 Then the congregation shall judge between the slayer and the revenger of blood according to these judgments: 25 And the congregation shall deliver the slayer out of the hand of the revenger of blood, and the congregation shall restore him to the city of his refuge, whither he was fled: and he shall abide in it unto the death of the high priest, which was anointed with the holy oil. 26 But if the slayer shall at any time come without the border of the city of his refuge, whither he was fled; 27 And the revenger of blood find him without the borders of the city of his refuge, and the revenger of blood kill the slayer; he shall not be guilty of blood: 28 Because he should have remained in the city of his refuge until the death of the high priest: but after the death of the high priest the slayer shall return into the land of his possession. 29 So these *things* shall be for a statute of judgment unto you throughout your generations in all your dwellings. 30 Whoso killeth any person, the murderer shall be put to death by the mouth of witnesses: but one witness shall not testify against any person *to cause him* to die. 31 Moreover ye shall take no satisfaction [כפר] for the life of a murderer, which *is* guilty of death: but he shall be surely put to death. 32 And ye shall take no satisfaction for him that is fled to the city of his refuge, that he should come again to dwell in the land, until the death of the priest. 33 So ye shall not pollute the land wherein ye *are*: for blood it defileth the land: and the land cannot be cleansed of the blood that is shed therein, but by the blood of him that shed it.[81]

Deuteronomy 19:10–13:

10 That innocent blood be not shed in thy land, which the LORD thy God giveth thee *for* an inheritance, and *so* blood be upon thee. 11 But if any man hate his neighbour, and lie in wait for him, and rise up against him, and smite him mortally that he die, and fleeth into one of these cities: 12 Then the elders of his city shall send and fetch him thence, and deliver him into the hand of the avenger of blood, that he may die. 13 Thine eye shall not pity him, but thou shalt put away *the guilt of* innocent blood from Israel, that it may go well with thee.[82]

Presupposing the sanctity of human life, Moses urges the covenant community to revere "innocent blood," honoring the rights of the innocent. S.R. Driver remarks on the importance of honoring the innocent, to implicitly not protect the guilty:

That innocent blood be not shed . . . as it would be, if a man, not guilty of deliberate murder, were slain by the avenger of blood.[83]

81. *The King James Version*, electronic ed. (Accordance Bible Software, Oak-Tree Software, Inc., version 14, 2025), accessed July 21, 2025. Brackets inserted by the author.

82. *The King James Version*, electronic ed. (Accordance Bible Software, OakTree Software, Inc., version 14, 2025), accessed July 21, 2025.

83. S. R. Driver, *A Critical and Exegetical Commentary on Deuteronomy*, 3rd ed., International Critical Commentary (Edinburgh: T. & T. Clark, 1902), 232. "Innocent blood," as 21:8, 27:25, Jer. 7:6 *al.* Driver remarks on the texts that

The Hebrew Bible's procedural and substantive due process is explicit, "two or three" independent corroborating witnesses—not where one tells another and the echoing witness merely repeats hearsay—with independent, objective judges, is explicit.[84]

Procedural Due Process	Torah Precept	Judicial Objective
Multiple witnesses	Numbers 35:30	Ensure verifiable evidentiary base
Discern Negligence v. Malice Aforethought	Numbers 35:9–29	Prevent overcharging and hyper-sentencing
Judicial scrutiny — checks and balances	Deuteronomy 17:8–9	Formalize evidentiary process for legal fairness
No ransom, fine, compensation (or bribe)	Numbers 35:31	Ensure justice not only "for all" who can pay
Penalty for false, perjurious witnesses	Deuteronomy 19:15–21	Deter perjury/preempt fraud/stop slander

require protecting the innocent.

84. Frank E. Hirsch, "Assassination," in *The International Standard Bible Encyclopaedia*, ed. James Orr et al. (Chicago: The Howard-Severance Company, 1915) 288.

CONCLUSION

As a matter of both public record and public interest, the advocacy and rhetoric of vengeful violence must not be tolerated in a nation governed by law and conscience. The conscience of the nation must become addicted to truth, not coercion.

We believe in *E pluribus unum*—"out of many, one." And how do many become one, and stay that way? When our differences divide us, we close ranks by ballots, not bullets. We believe in persuasion, not perdition.

We believe in dialogue, not destruction.

We are Americans.

May ballots prevail over bullets, argument over aggression, and debate over death dealing. As the Rev. Dr. Martin Luther King Jr. so aptly preached, "We must learn to live together as brothers, or we will die together as fools."[1]

---

1. The Rev. Dr. Martin Luther King Jr., *Remaining Awake through a Great Revolution*, commencement address at Oberlin College, June 1965 cited in *A Testament of Hope: The Essential Writings of Martin Luther King, Jr.*, ed. James M. Washington (San Francisco: Harper & Row, 1986). See also his St. Louis speech (22 March 1964), *"Remaining Awake Through a Great Revolution,"* delivered at Oberlin College in June 1965, quoted directly in the *St. Louis Post-Dispatch*.

www.ingramcontent.com/pod-product-compliance
Lightning Source LLC
Chambersburg PA
CBHW070924270326
41927CB00011B/2706